Samuel Beckett's *Murphy*

A Critical Excursion

UNIVERSITY OF GEORGIA MONOGRAPHS, NO. 15

Samuel Beckett's *Murphy*

A Critical Excursion

By

ROBERT HARRISON

DEPARTMENT OF ENGLISH

UNIVERSITY OF GEORGIA

UNIVERSITY OF GEORGIA PRESS

ATHENS   1968

Contents

Introduction

THE purpose of this essay is to demonstrate the value of a diagrammatic approach to a specific problem in literary explication. In the pages that follow, a critical framework will be outlined and then put to use in an examination of Samuel Beckett's novel, *Murphy*.

No originality is claimed for such an approach to literature: ever since Plato divided the "good" into three categories and Aristotle analyzed the constituent elements of Greek drama, systems of classification have been standard weapons in the critic's arsenal. Nor should the particular method suggested here be in any way interpreted as representing a new or polemical attitude toward literature. There is no "new" criticism—there are only incessant realignments of pattern, shifts in emphasis from poem to public to poet, from matter to manner, from form to function, with each movement only revealing new figures on old grounds.

But occasionally things go astray on the route from theory to practice, and gaps appear between broad interpretations of the nature of literature and the practice of criticism. On the one hand, theorists are frequently more concerned with the truth-value of a critical system or its accommodation to a broader philosophical position than with its utility as a *modus operandi*, and on the other, the working critic is often a specialist or an *homme engagé*, and in his enthusiasm may be inclined to substitute the part for the whole, so that when any critical assertion is launched into his field from another quarter, he interprets it as a personal attack. In this manner literature becomes at times little more than a battleground for the deployment of hostile, often non-literary,

1

opinions. For this reason it would seem desirable to make some effort to isolate and identify the various orders of assertions which may be made about a literary work.

The basis of this framework is frankly derivative. It evokes the encyclopaedic spirit of the doctrine of the *multiplex sensus*, and was suggested by the approach taken by Northrop Frye in his *Anatomy of Criticism*.[1] The *multiplex sensus*, as employed critically by the Alexandrian Philo Judaeus and creatively by Dante, regards the literary work as a laminated structure—that is, as a unity composed of several discrete levels of signification. The doctrine was first used as a means for explicating apparent contradictions in the Bible by interpreting any given passage on four levels of meaning, ranging from the literal to the anagogical. But in the latter part of the Renaissance many critics discarded this system, which shared the general odium of mediaeval Platonism, and began, under the influence of Latin models, to concern themselves chiefly with the relationship of the work to the public, devoting most of their efforts to the study of persuasive technique and efficacy. Thus until the rise of Romanticism the view of the literary work as a unique aesthetic creation was by and large reduced to that mental shrug, the *je ne sais quoi*. Then, under the aegis of Romantic theory, criticism temporarily shelved the public aim of rhetorical efficacy and began to measure value on the yardstick of sincerity and the "powerful feelings" of the artist. So the mills of criticism grind away. As tradition is dispossessed by innovation, its virtues as well as its faults are haphazardly stowed away like double-breasted tuxedos, to reappear only when critical fashion has come full circle.

In the past, the pace of critical evolution has been rather leisurely; each age has had ample time to seed its dogma and watch them mature and decay before a general reversal in taste has cleared the ground for a successor. But with the twentieth century, simultaneously pursuing, overtaking, disengaging, and merging with one another like the evolutionary cavalry charge in Bergson's metaphor, come Freudians, Jungians, Marxists, Expressionists, Naturalists, Neo-Aristotelians, New Critics, and so on, each with their own axes to grind. At the present time, therefore, in the midst of all these shifting currents, an eclectic approach to literature seems particularly desirable.

Within the diagrammatic framework proposed here the literary work will be regarded as a product of three broad areas of meaning, which may be equated tentatively with (1) history, (2) art, and (3) idea. These terms are necessarily vague, since the areas they define are broad but finite universes of discourse designed to encompass, rather than limit, the types of propositions which may be made about a work of literature. Under each of these areas are subsumed the relevant aspects of the predicaments with which the critic customarily deals, such as form, character, symbol/motif, and style.

(1) *History*. In this area of meaning the work is to be viewed as *matter* in the sense of raw material, and as a product of tradition, whether historical, literary, or psychological. The relationship to be kept in mind here is that of the literary work to the past. In Aristotelian terms it is the work seen as *mythos;* in Jungian terms it is the work seen as a manifestation of the collective unconscious or racial memory; in the Platonic sense it may be seen as Recollection. Within this sphere of reference, it will be observed that the predicament of form includes the conventional idea of *story* or *plot* in the sense meant by the assertion "There are no new plots," and lends itself to the study of genres and mythic patterns in literature. Therefore form will also include the archetypal construct, what Joyce has called the "monomyth."[2] This identification of form as matter helps define the limits of the next predicament, character. This is the bailiwick of the Freudian and Jungian critic, as well as the literary historian. Characters may be seen here as representatives of the archetypes as well as descendants of earlier literary and historical personages. Idiosyncrasies of character are not to be considered within this area—what is pertinent here is the typical and the archetypical. The same rules hold for symbols and motifs: it is the recurrence of tradition, history, and myth that concerns the critic here. Finally, the predicament of style in this context asks questions about sources and influences. It may be observed that the relationship of the artist to his work enters in here;

nevertheless, biographical data must be used with a great deal
of caution, and the critic must be aware that only those
facts which contribute to an understanding of the literary
work can be admitted as valid evidence. To put it simply,
the writer's life matters only insofar as it documents his
writing.

(2) *Art.* Here the literary work will be seen from an
aesthetic point of view as *manner* or invention. The question
is no longer what is it made of? or from what does it
derive? but how is it made? In the Platonic sense this view
may be equated with the function of the Soul and Understanding. The predicament of form, seen before as mythic
pattern and historical event, is now to be considered as a
non-referential element of aesthetic design, as the artistic
use made of mythic and traditional patterns of action. In
other words, it is the dramatic shape of the work. For
example: in *Ulysses,* form as matter refers to the heroic
myth archetypically and to Homer's adaptation of it historically. But here form concerns the dramatic movement
of Stephen Dedalus, Leopold and Molly Bloom, and the
citizens of Dublin on the 16th of June 1904. Now it may be
argued that the significance of the form of *Ulysses* will be lost
to a great degree if constant association is not maintained
in the reader's mind between the events of the novel and
their mythic and Homeric correspondences. Exactly: for the
distinction made between the areas described here is not
intended to produce any compartmentalization of viewpoint
toward the work—on the contrary, it is for the purpose
of holding in suspension the various orders of critical assertions that this framework is proposed. To say that Leopold
Bloom is an Irish advertisement canvasser of Jewish ancestry
as well as an avatar of Odysseus implies no contradiction;
but it does indicate the need to recognize that the two identities exist in differing orders of discourse. Therefore, within
the aesthetic area referential elements of character are not
to be considered. The fact that Joseph Bloom was a dentist
in Dublin who, like Leopold, once lived at 38 Lombard
Street, will be of interest to the literary detective as a
contribution to the understanding of the novel as history, but
is irrelevant here. Even the earlier appearance of Stephen

Dedalus in *A Portrait of the Artist as a Young Man* may be seen to document the matter of *Ulysses*, but it in no way predetermines the aesthetic use of the character of Stephen Dedalus in the latter work. Character here is an instrument of aesthetic pattern: the people in a novel oppose, complement, define one another; they unite within the closed universe of the work, and they act out the design of the plot. In a similar manner, symbol and motif may be seen as elements of rhythm and pattern, of what the Elizabethan rhetoricians called *enargia*. The function of motif seen aesthetically is described by E. M. Forster in this way:

[The novel] should accrete round a single topic, situation, gesture, which should occupy the characters and provide a plot, and should also fasten up the novel on the outside—catch its scattered statements in a net, make them cohere like a planet, and swing through the skies of memory. A pattern must emerge, and anything that emerged from the pattern must be pruned off as wanton distraction.[3]

Like the other predicaments, style is also non-referential in this context. Northrop Frye makes the following distinction between *literal* and *descriptive* meaning:

In literature, questions of fact or truth are subordinated to the primary literary aim of producing a structure of words for its own sake, and the sign-values of symbols are subordinated to their importance as a structure of interconnected motifs. Wherever we have an autonomous verbal structure of this kind, we have literature. Wherever this autonomous structure is lacking, we have language, words used instrumentally to help human consciousness do or understand something else.[4]

At this stage, then, style is understood as an instrument of "literal" meaning and a constituent of literature, as opposed to language. From this it follows that any statement as to whether or not a piece of writing is "literature" must be based on evidence drawn from this area of signification. Incidentally, it is at this level that style comes nearest the condition of music.

(3) *Idea.* This level of meaning regards the literary work as a vehicle for the presentation of intellectual viewpoints. As at the historical level, the stress here is on content, the

difference being that content is now seen as expression rather than impression. In other words, it is the intellectual use that the raw material of language is put to. In the Aristotelian sense the work is seen as *dianoia;* in the Platonic, as Spirit. The question to be asked of the predicaments here is no longer what? or how? but what for? Form may be identified in this area with *fable,* with action which serves to illustrate an idea. This is the level on which allegorical meaning appears; in scholastic terms it is the level that the "language of accommodation" renders in concrete terms.[5] As well as representing the ideational interplay of character and incident, form here also describes the shapes of ideas. Beckett illustrates this use of form when he quotes the following passage from Augustine: "Do not despair; one of the thieves was saved. Do not presume; one of the thieves was damned." Similarly, characters are no longer regarded as archetypes or as *dramatis personae,* but as representatives of specific intellectual outlooks. It is not difficult to find this use of character in literature; it has been the organizing principle of satire since the time of Menippus. As Frye points out:

> The Menippean satire deals less with people as such than with mental attitudes. Pedants, bigots, cranks, parvenus, virtuosi, enthusiasts, rapacious and incompetent professional men of all kinds, are handled in terms of their occupational approach to life as distinct from their social behavior.[6]

Symbols and motifs are now treated as functional elements in the intellectual design of the work. Unlike their counterparts in the areas of history and aesthetics, here they normally have well-defined sign functions; that is, they are recognized as possessing specific intellectual referents. Applicable at this level is the Renaissance definition of the symbol as a significant abstraction, portrayed through vivid concretions, which elucidates, discriminates, differentiates and defines by means of logical similitude. This is not to say that the "significant abstraction" for which the symbol stands will always be simple, for the reference may be quite complicated with aesthetic and archetypal significance, so that its logical core is difficult to perceive. (Witness, for example, the central symbol in Virginia Woolf's *To The Lighthouse.*) Style now becomes associated with the techniques of persuasion, and may be described with the terms of formal rhetoric; especially useful in this area are those critical methods growing out of the study of the relationship between the work and its audience. It may be observed that style is now "descriptive" in Frye's sense: that is, its referent is no longer the closed system of the work itself, but rather the idea expressed.

This then is a rough sketch of the critical framework to be employed in the following pages. At this point I wish to make it clear that the three broad areas of signification outlined here are not to be regarded as forming any sort of hierarchy of relative importance. Unlike the vertical structure of the traditional *multiplex sensus*, no ranking is to be inferred from the order of presentation: the customary sequence of *Stoff-Form-Gehalt* has been followed solely for the sake of convenience. In the final analysis, each work of literature must be allowed to determine its relationship to the various areas of meaning and dictate the uses to be made of them.

Several objections may be raised to this sort of diagrammatic framework. The most obvious of these is the one which may be advanced by the dedicated student of any school of literature—that each movement establishes its own standards, which then become the sole articles of faith relevant to any criticism of it. This attitude finds its foundation in the assumption that a literary work fails or succeeds solely to the extent that it reflects, or does not reflect, the purpose its creator had in mind at the time of writing it. Thus, ultimately, the author himself becomes the only qualified critic of his work, and his personal aesthetic convictions and *Weltanschauung* the only sources of authority. Who but Joyce Kilmer can say that "Trees" was not intended to be an exceptionally bad poem? But when art and criticism promote one another, they often become so mutually dependent that criticism sacrifices through commitment the advantages of detachment, and literature loses the disinterested perspective which tradition alone can provide. The *reductio ad absurdem* of this situation may be seen in the so-called "aesthetic happenings" and their apologists; here militant ignorance has become handmaiden of the boldly meaningless.

The objection might also be raised that it is more desirable for the critic to specialize, to examine literature from a single viewpoint, rather than to try to master a broad range of critical approaches. There is a good deal to be said in favor of this argument, but the danger remains that the critic may become more attached to his method than his subject. The pernicious tendency here is to see a literary work as *just* this or that, and nothing more; that is, to stake out a claim to a single, limited view and then endeavor to subordinate the whole range of critical propositions to it, rather than the work itself. Perhaps this indicates that the critic should at times limit himself horizontally rather than vertically—that he should bring to bear the greatest possible variety of critical approaches upon a rather narrow area of literature, rather than travel from work to work with a single set of tools.

But the most telling argument against this sort of framework is that it is merely a tempest in a teapot, that the good critic always plies his trade eclectically and is fully aware of the orders of assertions he makes, without having to resort to any cumbersome diagrammatic approach. This argument concludes it is unnecessary to formulate that which is already common knowledge and public domain. And it should be: but the fact is that since few works of criticism can be exhaustive enough to display more than a limited view of a literary work, difficulties often arise, and perfectly valid sets of critical propositions become strangely opposed to one another. Frequently it is not that the wrong answers are given, but that different kinds of questions are asked. In other words, by failing to acknowledge the simultaneous presence of a number of discrete areas of meaning that inform any given work, critics often set in opposition assertions of quite different orders. Such assertions are like unsuccessful metaphors: lacking a common predicament, they stand neither in contradiction nor conjunction, but remain in eternal abeyance.

CHAPTER I

Form

FIRST, a summary of what "happens" in *Murphy*. As the book opens, the reader is introduced to Murphy, an indigent bachelor of unspecified but not advanced age. He sits naked and bound in a rocking-chair near the window of his condemned flat in West Brompton, a suburb of Greater London, musing over his recent philosophical studies under a Cork County man by the name of Neary. The telephone rings, interrupting his reverie; on the line is Celia, Murphy's mistress and would-be fiancée. She tells him she has got his Nativity (Murphy is to be reached only through the stars) and is bringing it to him. He tries in vain to dissuade her. She hangs up and he returns to his rocking.

In the next scene we meet Celia and learn through a bedside dialogue with her grandfather, an invalid kiting enthusiast named Kelly, that she is an eminently nubile ex-prostitute who, in order to make her fondest dreams come true, must persuade Murphy to marry her and go to work. For this purpose she has engaged the technical assistance of a cut-rate swami in Berwick Street to cast a Nativity which will demonstrate to him the desirability of home, job, and family. Late that evening (12 September 1935) Celia goes to Murphy's flat. On the stairs she bumps into a man smelling strongly of whisky, who we learn later is Neary's henchman, Cooper. She finds Murphy in an inverted position (his rocker has overturned), rights him and gives him the Nativity. It serves its purpose, for after some hesitation he seems ready to set out on the jobpath.

In Dublin a week later, Murphy's ex-mentor Neary is rescued from the Civic Guard by a man named Wylie, after having been apprehended for wantonly dashing his head against the buttocks of the statue of Cuchulain in the Central Post Office. Wylie takes Neary to a nearby café and elicits from him the following story: Neary is in love with a Miss Counihan, who is in love with Murphy. But since no word has come from Murphy for the past four months, Miss Counihan has agreed to admit Neary to her graces, on the condition that he offer proof of Murphy's death or permanent desertion. Accepting the challenge Neary has sent his *âme damnée* Cooper to look for Murphy in London. Meanwhile Neary has vainly tried his luck with Miss Counihan. This morning Neary has received two telegrams from Cooper, the first reading FOUND STOP LOOK SLIPPY STOP COOPER and the second LOST STOP STOP WHERE YOU ARE COOPER. Neary is at his wits' end. Wylie suggests that Neary go to London himself, but Neary is reluctant to do this, for fear that he might be seen there by his second deserted wife, Ariadne *née* Cox.

Meanwhile Celia and Murphy have taken a flat in Brewery Road and entered upon the new life. Every day Murphy goes out ostensibly to look for work while Celia waits in the rocking-chair and listens to the constant pacing of the "old boy" in the room directly above. On Friday, 11 October, while passing an idle moment in the British Museum, Murphy encounters Austin Ticklepenny, homosexual, ex-pot poet from the County of Dublin, and at present male nurse at a private asylum, the Magdalen Mental Mercyseat. Since Ticklepenny seems displeased with his current line of work, Murphy volunteers to take over his job at the institution. Ticklepenny agrees to this and they part. Murphy proceeds to the Cockpit in Hyde Park, where he loses his noonday ration of cookies to a dachshund named Nelly, property of Rosie Dew, a spiritual medium. In a brief digression, Miss Dew is followed to her home and her relationship to her benefactor, Lord Gall of Wormwood, is amplified. Murphy leaves the Cockpit and returns to find Celia in a state of shock. The "old boy" upstairs has cut his throat.

Now the action moves back to October 7 in Dublin. Neary has departed for London, leaving Miss Counihan in the more than solicitous care of Wylie. Cooper (whom Neary has dis-

charged in a fit of pique for losing Murphy) enters Miss
Counihan's hotel room unannounced and finds the couple in
compromising circumstances, but his indignation is soon
mollified by Wylie's timely application of whisky. He tells
of his adventures in London. After finding Murphy in the
overturned rocking-chair Cooper assumed that he had been
murdered, so he took the tube for Wapping and there drank
for a week. When sufficiently recovered from the shock,
he hurried back to West Brompton, pausing on the way to
wire Neary that Murphy had been found. But upon arrival
he saw that the mew in which Murphy lived was being
carried away, brick by brick, and immediately wired Neary
that Murphy had been lost again. At this, Neary had come
to London and fired him.

Wylie enlists Cooper in his own cause (Miss Counihan)
and proposes that the three of them set out immediately for
London. Privately he plans to remove Neary as an obstacle by
informing Ariadne *née* Cox of Neary's presence in the city.

Now the action returns to Brewery Road. After unsuccessful efforts to cheer up Celia, Murphy leaves for his new
job at the Magdalen Mental Mercyseat. When he does not
return, Celia moves upstairs into the room vacated by the
"old boy" and waits. The following Saturday, as Celia is
strolling in Kensington Gardens, Cooper (now employed by
Wylie and Miss Counihan) recognizes her and follows her to
the flat in Brewery Road.

In the meantime Murphy has relieved Ticklepenny of his
duties in the M.M.M. and settled in a garret at the asylum.
The garret, though less than palatial, would be an empyrean
to Murphy but for its one drawback, the lack of heat. To
correct this fault Ticklepenny installs a spatchcock gas radiator,
linked to a disused jet in the w.c. below by means of a series
of discarded feed tubes. The heating problem solved, Murphy
leaves the grounds of the M.M.M. only once thereafter, to
retrieve his rocker from Brewery Road.

Next the narrative returns to the domestic intrigues of
Wylie, Neary, and Miss Counihan. Miss Counihan, playing her
hole card, withholds her charms from both her admirers and
bribes Cooper to report to her every day before he goes
to Wylie. Also, behind Wylie's back she accosts Neary and

makes a clean breast of her affair with Wylie. Likewise, Wylie browbeats Cooper into reporting all news of Murphy to him first, and, unknown to Miss Counihan, confesses all to Neary. Cooper, the perfect double agent, feels no awkwardness whatever at this state of affairs and makes full and frank reports to each of his employers in order of convenience. Neary, who by now has recovered from his itch for Miss Counihan and desires only to regain the friendship of Murphy, takes to his bed and awaits further developments.

Five people now need Murphy. Celia needs him for his love, Miss Counihan for his "surgical quality," Neary for a friend, Cooper because he is paid to, and Wylie because he must prove him unfaithful in order to win over Miss Counihan.

Cooper, having spotted Celia, reports the news to his principals, who both send him in search of Ariadne *née* Cox and then converge on Neary. They call a temporary truce and set out to Brewery Road to find Murphy. Here they meet Celia and learn that Murphy has once again vanished. All this takes place on Sunday, 20 October.

At the M.M.M. Murphy has now gone on night duty. After an evening of intermittent rounds and chess with Mr. Endon, a schizophrenic with tendencies to asphyxia, he retires to his garret, lights his stove, ties himself in his chair and rocks himself into nescience. The flame dies out, but the gas goes on. "Soon his body was quiet."[1]

The following scene brings together Celia, Miss Counihan, Neary, Wylie, and Cooper at the mortuary of the M.M.M., where they identify the remains of Murphy. Miss Counihan is satisfied, not having lost Murphy to Celia; Neary is satisfied, seeing in Celia a potential anodyne for his grief at the loss of both Murphy and Miss Counihan; Cooper is satisfied, having found his man; and Wylie is satisfied, having correctly predicted that Celia would lead them to Murphy. Only Celia is dissatisfied.

After Murphy's body has been duly identified, his last testament is read. His wishes are that his mind, body, and soul be burnt and placed in a paper bag and brought to the Abbey Theatre, Lr. Abbey Street, Dublin, and without pause into . . .

the necessary house . . . on the right as one goes down into the
pit, and . . . that the chain be there pulled upon them. . . . (269)

Neary now pays off his assistants, arranges to have Murphy's body cremated, and instructs Cooper to "dump it any-
where." (272) Meanwhile, Wylie, having money in his pocket,
disengages himself from the now clinging Miss Counihan.
Likewise Neary, learning from Cooper that Ariadne *née* Cox
has committed suicide and consequently he is free to show
himself in London without fear, tips his hat politely to Miss
Counihan and takes his leave.

Cooper waits at the Mercyseat until Murphy has been
reduced to a portable parcel of ashes, then adjourns to the
local public house. In the course of the evening's fun he scouts
the packet at a fellow reveler and "by closing time the body,
mind, and soul of Murphy were freely distributed over the
floor of the saloon." (275)

The final scene takes place three days later, on 26 October.
Celia, who has returned to her former profession, wheels
her grandfather to Kensington Gardens for his afternoon of
kiting. His kite soars higher and higher, out of sight, and
the string breaks. The old man totters to his feet and stumbles
down the slope of the Round Pond in pursuit of the trailing
end of kitestring. Celia catches him at the brink of the pond,
restores him to his wheelchair, and pushes him homeward
as the park rangers call *All out*.

When seen in a traditional perspective, the first sentence of *Murphy*, "The sun shone, having no alternative, on
the nothing new," (1) hints at the sort of pattern we may
expect to find throughout the book, one of intellectualized
description employing the overtly ironic view of Menippean
satire. This genre uses plot primarily for the development
of ideas, just as it uses character to embody stereotyped
outlooks. However, the distinction between the literary use
of an idea and its inherent truth-value should be kept constantly in mind—for herein lies the difference between literal
and descriptive meaning. For example, assertions such as
Wylie's "The horse leech's daughter is a closed system. Her
quantum of wantum cannot vary" (57) contribute little to
the *dianoia* of the book, but they do serve to point up the

tension between physical and intellectual reality, which has always been a mainstay of this literary type.

Another trademark of Menippean satire is its external view of character. It may seem at first glance that Beckett takes us into the mind of his hero—and so he does, in a sense. But through meticulous control of the narrative viewpoint, achieved by means of several stylistic sleights-of-hand, he manages to keep the reader continuously aware of Murphy's thought processes; in other words, we do not take part in Murphy's thoughts—we see the narrator seeing them.

The conventions of satire often require action to take place on the diminutive scale of the ironic mode. In the same manner that tragedy ultimately aspires to religious myth, so the humorous vision of satire gravitates toward the sub-human. True, Murphy is a hero of sorts, but one of a distinctly inferior order, trapped in a universe he is unable to control, and his power of action is superior only to that of the later Beckett protagonists. But further discussion of Murphy himself will be deferred to the treatment of character, so it must suffice for the moment to say that Murphy is an ironic quester.

This brings us to the next aspect of form as history—its mythic pattern. At the surface of the work lies the tableau of incident and detail which goes to make up the "story"; beneath it operate those motifs which sort out the superficial data and arrange them in aesthetically coherent patterns. But still deeper, at the level of mythic form, the same events may be seen in terms of the four stages of the heroic quest: descent, death, return, and apotheosis. Here the idosyncrasies of plot disappear, and only the universal and archetypal remain. At the level of mythic form all works of narrative fiction trace out the arcs of their movement on the circumference of a common circle, and differences are indicated only by the sector of the circle described. The cyclical myth has been summarized in this way:

> The mythological hero, setting forth from his commonday hut or castle, is lured, carried away, or else voluntarily proceeds, to the threshold of adventure. There he encounters a shadow presence that guards the passage. The hero may defeat or conciliate this power and go alive into the kingdom of the

dark (brother-battle, dragon-battle; offering, charm), or be slain by the opponent and descend in death (dismemberment, cruci-fixion). Beyond the threshold, then, the hero journeys through a world of unfamiliar yet strangely intimate forces, some of which severely threaten him (tests), some of which give magical aid (helpers). When he arrives at the nadir of the mythological round, he undergoes a supreme ordeal and gains his reward. The triumph may be represented as the hero's sexual union with the goddess-mother of the world (sacred marriage), his recognition by the father-creator (father atonement), his own divinization (apotheosis), or again—if the powers have remained unfriendly to him—his theft of the boon he came to gain (bride-theft, fire-theft); intrinsically it is an expansion of consciousness and therewith of being (illumination, transfiguration, freedom). The final work is that of the return. If the powers have blessed the hero, he now sets forth under their protection (emissary); if not, he flees and is pursued (transformation flight, obstacle flight). At the return threshold the transcendental powers must remain behind; the hero re-emerges from the kingdom of dread (return, resurrection). The boon that he brings restores the world (elixir).[2]

Thus in mythic terms the plots of the *Odyssey*, the *Divine Comedy*, and Kafka's *The Castle* may be diagrammed as follows:

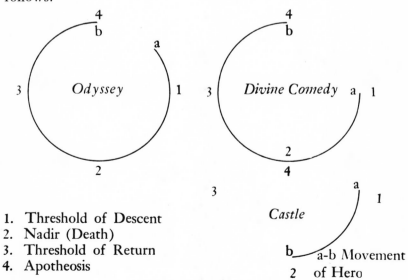

1. Threshold of Descent
2. Nadir (Death)
3. Threshold of Return
4. Apotheosis

Now the complete mythic cycle may be defined as the movement of a hero or quester which describes more than 180° of a great circle beginning in the everyday world and terminating with his return to the world reborn as a new man (or god), bearing proofs of his success. But when the quest takes place within the ironic mode, it is obvious that the hero's power of action is severely restricted—the conventions of the mode preclude the possibility of anything resembling apotheosis. Therefore, when examining the mythic outline of the ironic quest, the reader must be sensitive to the subtlest shifts of position. At the end of Kafka's *Trial*, for example, a faint glimmer of hope may be detected when "ein Licht aufzuckt, so fuhren die Fensterflügel eines Fensters dort auseinander, ein Mensch, schwach und dünn in der Ferne und Höhe, beugte sich mit einem Ruck weit vor und streckte die Arme noch weiter aus."[3] So it is with *Murphy*. Because of the limitations placed on the ironic mode, it might appear at first glance that no cyclical movement occurs, but one must bear in mind that each mode has its own standards; one cannot expect the ironic hero's triumph to be measured in any but ironic terms—unlike Hercules, Murphy has no invitation to the Olympian banquet. Perhaps Belacqua's bliss is for him a more suitable token of success.

In mythic terms, the only significant movement in the book is that of Murphy himself; the other characters merely serve as helping or hindering or commenting foils and can be seen as stock figures of the quest. In an outline of Murphy's mythic movement three way-stations may be observed: Brewery Road, the M.M.M., and the public house to which Cooper commits his ashes. Incidentally, the transitional nature of all places for Murphy is brought into sharp focus here. The flat in Brewery Road is located between Pentonville Prison and the Metropolitan Cattle Market (slavery and slaughter); one of his favorite lounging places on the jobpath lies between the Milton House and the tripe factory (sickness and disembowelment); and even the Magdalen Mental Mercyseat is situated between two counties.

When Murphy appears on page 1 he is already near the threshold of descent: he is about to be evicted from his mew, Nearyan heart control has failed to give him respite, and even his rocking-chair is treacherously unstable. Through no effort of his own, he gradually approaches the brink. The final shove is given him by Suk, Celia, and the "new life."

Brewery Road represents the moment of crisis for Murphy. In spite of his daily round of sensual pleasure with Celia, Murphy dies into life here, in a way Keats never meant it. While living with Celia he becomes more and more a man and less than ever Murphy. But then the "old boy" upstairs commits suicide and indirectly provides Murphy with his challenge to the quest. Celia is so distracted by the event that she can no longer persuade him to stay, so Murphy begins his descent into the dark.

The distortion produced by the ironic mode is nowhere so evident as it is here. The hero's journey is normally seen as a progression consummated by his return and reintegration with society as the new king or "master of two worlds," the human and the divine. But with Murphy all signs must be changed. His quest is, in psychological terms, a regression;[4] society is his waste land, and only in an insane asylum can he find hope for resurrection.

At the M.M.M. Murphy crosses the threshold of adventure and reaches the nadir of his journey. On the surface (and even at his own level of perception, considerably beneath the surface) he fails here too. He finds himself exiled even in the world of the microcosmopolitans, and exile is the one thing Murphy has not learned to live with. At the plot level there is nothing left for him but death and dissolution.

Nevertheless, the machinery of mythic form rolls on: metamorphosed, Murphy is removed from the M.M.M. by Cooper (who must be seen here as an agent of the gods) and symbolically united with the universe. In this manner his quest is completed.

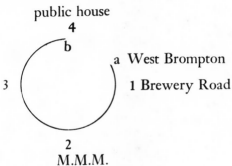

public house
4

b

a West Brompton

3

1 Brewery Road

2
M.M.M.

In contrast to Murphy, Celia never succeeds in escaping the round of everyday existence. For one thing, her outlook is essentially pre-Murphyan; her "new life" is Murphy's death as a quester. Also, because of her attachment to humanity, represented by the "old boy" upstairs, she can never accept the withdrawal and self-dissolution demanded of questers. Celia sets out on the right road, but for the wrong reasons: because she loves Murphy and is tired of her trade, she embarks on the *vita nuova*. But as she soon learns, new lives cannot be bought cheap. During Murphy's daily absence on the jobpath, she begins to follow him slowly along the questpath. But her progress (that is, regress) is arrested by the death of the "old boy" and her subsequent loss of Murphy. At this point she fails to pick up the gauntlet of the quest and languishes in the static role of the death-wisher. She remains frozen at the threshold of the quest until Murphy's death, then returns to her grandfather and the old life. Thus, in terms of mythic form, Celia's movement is that of the potential quester who refuses to accept the challenge.

As indicated in the introduction to this essay, the questions asked of form in the aesthetic area are chiefly those relating to dramatic structure. Here we may see the action of the characters as a counterbalance of stasis and movement. The supporting players—Neary, Wylie, Miss Counihan, Celia, Ticklepenny, Mr. Endon, and Cooper—seem to oscillate rather than progress. Where Murphy has a quest, no matter how ironic it may be, the minor characters in the book have only an endless succession of identical desires. In pursuit of these they continually form conjunctions and oppositions among one another, only to wind up exactly where they started from. Neary, for instance:

Of such was Neary's love for Miss Dwyer, who loved a Flight-Lieutenant Elliman, who loved a Miss Farren of Ringsakiddy, who loved a Father Fitt of Ballinclashet, who in all sincerity was bound to acknowledge a certain vocation for a Mrs. West of Passage, who loved Neary. (5)

The nature of such alliances is properly a matter of character and theme, but their kinetic function may be noted here. While the minor characters appear to be in constant motion and Murphy is throughout most of the book physically and geographically at rest, the aesthetic effect is the opposite of this. For Murphy, unlike the others, has somewhere to go.

A similar distinction may be observed with regard to time. In the narration and the dialogue of the minor characters, constant reference is made to clock time, time of day, phases of the moon, tides, and so on. Yet there is one character who seldom if ever knows what time it is—Murphy. Even the cuckoo-clock he hears from his flat strikes between twenty and thirty, like the English clock in Ionesco's *Cantatrice chauve*. For Murphy's quest has brought him outside the dimension of time, while everyone else in the book (except, of course, Mr. Endon) is bound to its wheel.

The following breakdown by scenes may be useful here:

scene	page	characters
1	1	Murphy alone in his rocking-chair
2	4	Flashback to Neary and Murphy
3	7	Telephone call from Celia to Murphy
4	10	Celia and Mr. Kelly
5	26	Celia and Murphy
6	42	Wylie and Neary
7	63	Exposition: Murphy and Celia at Brewery Road
8	68	Celia and Miss Carridge
9	80	Murphy and Vera at the lunch counter
10	84	Murphy and Ticklepenny
11	97	Murphy and Rosie Dew
12	107	Exposition: Murphy's mind
13	114	Exposition: Kelly, Neary, Wylie, Miss Counihan, Cooper
14	132	Celia and Miss Carridge
15	137	Celia and Murphy
16	143	Celia and Miss Carridge
17	150	Exposition: Celia alone in Kensington Gardens
18	156	Exposition: the M.M.M.; Murphy and Ticklepenny
19	195	Exposition: Miss Counihan, Wylie, Neary, Cooper
20	203	Miss Counihan and Cooper
21	204	Wylie and Cooper

scene	page	characters
22	207	Neary, Wylie, Miss Counihan
23	224	Neary, Wylie, Miss Counihan
24	229	Neary, Wylie, Miss Counihan, Celia, Miss Carridge
25	241	Murphy and Mr. Endon
26	251	Murphy alone in his rocking-chair
27	254	Neary, Wylie, Miss Counihan, Celia, Cooper, Ticklepenny, Clinch
28	275	Cooper and Murphy
29	277	Celia and Mr. Kelly

A number of interesting patterns emerge in this scene division of the book. In terms of the dramatic deployment of characters two consistent tendencies are apparent: whereas the minor characters come together in progressively larger groupings, so that by the time of Murphy's death all of them are present at the M.M.M., Murphy and Celia remain comparatively aloof. Celia is of course closer to society than Murphy (she must always "have" someone), but until Murphy leaves her she is seen in relation only to him, her grandfather, and Miss Carridge, and all her scenes up to this point are duologues. Throughout the book Murphy is a loner (with one exception: when Ticklepenny introduces him to Bim Clinch), and most of his speeches are soliloquies played off against whoever happens to be his dramatic foil at the moment. Only with Celia does Murphy ever enter into genuine conversation.

The minor characters play two sorts of roles: they serve to "swell the progress" by representing the thematic worlds of the book, and they act as sounding-boards for the narrator, Murphy, and Celia. The dramatic interrelationship of the various characters at this level of inquiry may be represented in the following diagram:

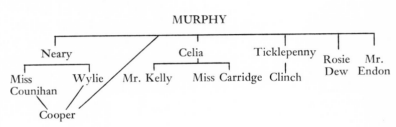

A symmetrical pattern informs the events of the book: minor characters are picked up one at a time, gathered into groups through their common need for Murphy, then once again dispersed as soon as he dies and the *raison d'être* of their society disintegrates. But more striking is the balanced arrangement of scenes given to Murphy and Celia: at his first and last appearances Murphy sits alone in his rocking-chair, trying to escape from something; at beginning and end Celia is seen with her grandfather. And each of them is given a brief thematic exposition occurring roughly at the mid-points of their journeys: scene 12 is a detailed treatment of Murphy's mind and scene 17, by linking Celia with Kensington Gardens and Mr. Kelly, both sums up her past and anticipates her future. But in general the shape of the action offers little novelty; of more interest here are the technical devices used to cement this basic form into an aesthetic unity.

First, Beckett keeps his subject at close tether. From beginning to end structural cohesion is emphasized; nineteen of the twenty-nine scenes listed above are played by only two persons, and in most of these active and passive roles are explicitly assigned to each of the characters. Five of these are bedside scenes, in which Mr. Kelly, Murphy, Neary, Celia and Mr. Endon are deprived of movement; in three Murphy is bound to his chair and cannot move; and throughout most of the final scene of the book Mr. Kelly is restricted to his wheelchair. Only twice is Murphy the moving actor in a scene: when he tries to cheer up Celia and when he goes to sit at the feet of Mr. Endon—the rest of the time other characters come to him. Although Murphy may be seen thematically and aesthetically as a moving figure, spatially and dramatically he remains for the most part at rest. Likewise, Celia is more often passive than active. At the ends of this scale stand Cooper, eternally in meaningless motion, and Mr. Endon, who cannot be permitted more than limited motion, because to move is to alter and thereby lessen in perfection.

Also serving to throw light on the aesthetic unity of the book are the frequent cross-references made by the narrator. For example, when Miss Counihan sits down on Neary's bed: "In a somewhat similar way Celia had sat on Mr. Kelly's bed,

and on Murphy's, though Mr. Kelly had had his shirt on."
(208) And on first view of Murphy in his rocking-chair:
"Slowly he felt better, astir in his mind, in the freedom of
that light and dark that did not clash, nor alternate, nor fade
nor lighten except to their communion, as described in section
six." (9) And in linking Cooper's first sight of Celia with
Celia's of Cooper: "Cooper entered, found Murphy in the
appalling position described in section three. . . ." (121)

The ironic distance established between narrator and
characters lends itself well to a tightly-knit dramatic structure. This may be observed in the scene- and stage-directions
interposed from time to time throughout the action. For
example, a formulaic pattern is used to introduce indirect discourse. It is first seen as Celia begins to tell her grandfather
how she met Murphy: "Celia's account, expurgated, accelerated, improved and reduced, of how she came to have to
speak of Murphy, gives the following." (12) This formula
appears next as Neary is about to explain to Wylie the events
leading up to his deplorable behavior in the Dublin General
Post Office, and still again when Cooper tells Miss Counihan
and Wylie how Neary fired him. But when Murphy's turn
comes, the issue is "lovingly simplified and perverted." (178)
The thematic key to this device is given finally, as Neary
tells a story in full: "When Neary had finished it was dark
in the room. Simplicity is as slow as a hearse and as long as a
last breakfast." (233)

At times the narrator wholeheartedly assumes the role of
stage director. He cues the players: "Enter Cooper." (118),
and places them on their marks: "All four are now in position.
They will not move from where they now are until they
find a formula, a *status quo* agreeable to all." (233) And
occasionally he provides detailed stage-directions: when Miss
Counihan comes to call on Neary, his hot water bottle bursts,
"so that water is oozing towards the centre of the floor
throughout the scene that follows." (208) Twice he even
goes so far as to introduce commentary on the inevitable
ending of the story. (227, 235)

These constant reminders of the ironic distance separating
narrator and subject operate throughout the action like the
zoom lens of a camera, expanding from microscopic scrutiny

to a God's eye panorama of mankind. In the following passage, for example, stage directions are given and the scale radically magnified at the same time. Murphy has just finished telling his triple pun to Celia: "The little scene was over, if scene it could be called. There was a long silence, Celia forgiving Murphy for having spoken roughly to her, Miss Counihan, Wylie and Cooper breaking their fast on the Liverpool-London express." (139)[5]

Conversely, in Chapter VI the narrator steps back into close range to document Murphy's mental processes. In a dramatic sense this chapter may be seen as an interlude between acts: Murphy has just returned to Brewery Road to find Celia spreadeagled on the bed and learned that the "old boy" has killed himself. Here, in the finest traditions of the ironic mode, the narrator launches an expository digression and transfers the reader's interest from plot to theme. Then at the end of this essay he closes formally and returns to the action.

Where form unites with idea, it is particularly important that the critic recognize to what extent sound appraisals of value may be made about the thematic "significance" of a work as literature. In this area of meaning, judgments must be made on the basis of the internal coherence of ideas, and not on their relation to any external body of theory or fact. Often critics short-circuit the effectiveness of their assertions by plugging irrelevant major premises into an author's syllogism and then finding fault with his conclusions; in doing this they only wind up shadowboxing with their favorite *bêtes noires*. If objections are to be raised to the theme of a work of fiction, they must be aimed carefully at flaws in its form.

The initial question to be asked of form here is: what is the exact nature of Murphy's quest? As the book opens he is sitting bound to his rocking-chair by seven scarves (or veils). He has adopted this practice because it both appeases his body and sets him free in his mind. It may be gathered from this that Murphy's quest is to be conducted within the limits of his consciousness. As he rocks and comes alive in his mind, he moves through the zones of light, half-light, and dark.

In the first were the forms with parallel, a radiant abstraction of the dog's life, the elements of physical experience available for a new arrangement. . . . In the second were the forms without parallel. Here the pleasure was contemplation. . . . Here was Belacqua bliss and others scarcely less precise. In both these zones of his private world Murphy felt sovereign and free, in the one to requite himself, in the other to move as he pleased from one unparalleled beatitude to another. . . . The third, the dark, was a flux of forms, a perpetual coming together and falling asunder of forms. . . . Here he was not free, but a mote in the dark of absolute freedom. He did not move, he was a point in the ceaseless unconditioned generation and passing away of time. (111-112)

In typical ironic fashion Murphy dreams an inversion of Descartes' celebrated dream of 10 November 1619. Murphy's movement may be seen as a symbolic journey through the three zones of consciousness signified by the mystic syllable *AUM*: waking, dream, and dreamless sleep. If this is true, then three of the stations of Murphy's journey may be marked off by Brewery Road, the M.M.M., and oblivion.

At this crossroads of form and theme, criticism also con-·cerns itself with the shapes of ideas. It may be worth while here to consider some of the peripheral elements of thematic form. In the epigrammatic colloquies of Neary, Wylie, and Miss Counihan, ideas pass by with blurring speed. Cartesian, Pythagorean, Augustinian ideas—their origins and truth-value are unimportant. It is only the form that matters. For example:

[Neary:]   Remember there is no triangle, however obtuse, but the circumference of some circle passes through its wretched vertices. Remember also one thief was saved. (213)

[Wylie:]   Who knows what dirty story, what even better dirty story, it may even be one we have not heard before, told at some colossal pitch of pure smut, beats at this moment in vain against our eardrums? (219)

Also, isomorphic sets of ideas help to point out the thematic gulf between characters—the "closed system," for example. To Murphy it means the little world, hermetically sealed off from the big; to Mr. Endon it does not *mean*—it *is*; but to

Wylie it signifies nothing more than the well with two buckets, one continually going down to be filled and the other just as persistently coming up to be emptied. A similar contrast may be seen as Murphy and Neary both draw on the metaphor of kicking to express their philosophical viewpoints. Ironically, Neary's extraverted *voltefesses* turns out to be in fact much more an offensive weapon than Murphy's introverted kick of retaliation.

One final element of theme must be mentioned here: the permutation. At regular intervals throughout the book the possibility of exhausting a series is considered. While Neary waits anxiously for word from Cooper, he passes his time in Mooney's public house,

moving slowly from one stool to another until he had completed the circuit of the counters, when he would start all over again in the reverse direction. He did not speak to the curates, he did not drink, . . . he did nothing but move slowly round the ring of counters, first in one direction, then in the other, thinking of Miss Counihan. (56)

Characteristically, to Neary the permutation is nothing more than a nervous tic, a way to make sure he will not stop thinking of Miss Counihan. On the other hand, to Murphy it is a source of perpetual delight. Like Schiller, he finds freedom only in the silent moment of contemplation that precedes an option, when all the possible alternatives of action may be viewed at once. Of this nature is Belacqua bliss.

At lunchtime Murphy goes to the Cockpit and sets his cookies out on the grass, preparatory to eating them.

They were the same as always, a Ginger, an Osborne, a Digestive, a Petit Beurre and one anonymous. He always ate the first-named last, because he liked it the best, and the anonymous first, because he thought it very likely the least palatable. The order in which he ate the remaining three was indifferent to him and varied irregularly from day to day. On his knees now before the five it struck him for the first time that these prepossessions reduced to a paltry six the number of ways in which he could make this meal. But this was to violate the very essence of assortment, this was red permanganate on the Rima of variety. Even if he conquered his prejudice against the anonymous, still there would be only twenty-four ways in which the biscuits could be eaten. But were he to take the final step and overcome his infatuation with the ginger, then the assortment would spring to life before him, dancing the radiant measure of its total permutability, edible in a hundred and twenty ways! (96-97)

Unhappily, the big world intervenes and Rosie Dew's dog opts for him. Then later, as Murphy prepares to assume his duties at the M.M.M., he starts another series; he tells Celia he will let her know if he has got the job "this evening . . . or if not this evening, to-morrow evening. Or if not to-morrow evening, the day after to-morrow evening." (141) And in the M.M.M., after Ticklepenny has rigged up a makeshift heater for his garret, Murphy briefly considers the possible ways he may bring the lighted gas-connection upstairs from its source in the w.c.

The final permutation is presented in full. Here the reader who has plodded through the sucking-stone interlude of *Molloy* or the description of Mr. Knott in *Watt* will find himself in familiar surroundings. When Mr. Endon slips out of his cell after the chess game, he drifts through the corridors of Skinner's House until he comes to the hypomaniac's pad, where Murphy finds him

ringing the changes on the various ways in which the indicator could be pressed and the light turned on and off. Beginning with the light turned off to begin with he had: lit, indicated, extinguished; lit, extinguished, indicated. Continuing then with the light turned on to begin with he had: extinguished, lit, indicated; extinguished, indicated, lit; indicated, extinguished and was seriously thinking of lighting when Murphy stayed his hand. (247)

This is a perfect example of the idea as pure form. Like the *Zweispringerspott* it is a mirror of Mr. Endon's closed system; when the last increment of the series is fitted into place, a mindtight sphere of meaninglessness comes into being. As the infinite computer grinds out its calculations, human intelligence is reduced to a pulp; the final wedge is driven between existence and understanding. In this manner, form is made to illustrate the principles of what Claude Mauriac has called

alittérature.[6] By closing the circle of permutation around a
thing or an act and still arriving at no significant assertion
about its meaning, Beckett opens up an abyss of incommunicability between narrator and reader and gives the nod
to the end of language itself. And in a still broader sense,
the closing of a finite circle of permutations signals symbolically the end of the universe.

In the great temple at Benares beneath the dome which marks
the center of the world, rests a brass plate in which are fixed
three diamond needles, each a cubit high . . . and as thick as the
body of a bee. On one of these needles, at the creation, God
placed sixty-four discs of pure gold, the largest disc resting on
the brass plate and the others getting smaller and smaller up
to the top one. This is the tower of Brahma. Day and night
unceasingly, the priest on duty transfers the discs from one
diamond needle to another, according to the fixed and immutable laws of Brahma, which require that the priest must
move only one disc at a time, and he must place these discs
on needles so that there never is a smaller disc below a larger
one. When all the sixty-four discs shall have been thus trans-
ferred from the needle on which, at the creation, God placed
them, to one of the other needles, tower, temple, and Brahmans
alike will crumble into dust, and with a thunderclap the world
will vanish.[7]

CHAPTER II

Character

Murphy

MURPHY is never "described" in the police-blotter sense of the word; only fragmentary hints suggest his physical appearance. He has eyes "cold and unwavering as a gull's," (2) a sallow complexion to match his lucky color, and he wears a black suit. His past is similarly vague. In an interview with her grandfather, Celia relates almost all we learn of Murphy's background:

He belonged to no profession or trade; came from Dublin . . . had one uncle, a Mr. Quigley, a well-to-do ne'er-do-well, resident in Holland, with whom he strove to correspond; did nothing that she could discern; sometimes had the price of a concert; believed that the future held great things in store for him; and never ripped up old stories. (17-18)

The character of Murphy seen as matter reveals a number of mythic likenesses. As indicated earlier, Murphy may be regarded as a quester moving through a field of more or less "flat" minor characters. Beckett himself remarks that "all the puppets in this book whinge sooner or later, except Murphy, who is not a puppet." (122) With the distortion of values that accompanies the ironic mode, the protagonist is customarily seen by society as a *pharmakos* or scapegoat, and becomes therefore a kind of anti-hero in worldly terms. So at the beginning of the book Murphy is living in a condemned mew (both senses of the word are fitting) from which he will soon be evicted.

Since in Western literature the archetypal *pharmakos* is Christ, the perfectly good man under sentence of death, it is hardly surprising that Murphy should be seen frequently as a Christ figure. When his rocking-chair overturns and Celia undoes the scarves about his body, "part by part he subsided, as the bonds that held him fell away, until he lay fully prostrate in the crucified position, heaving." (28) Here again we see the inversion produced by the ironic mode, for Murphy is not only crucified, but crucified upside down, in the manner of Saint Sécaire. Again, since Murphy left Ireland for London in February he has been seen by his friends but once, "on Maundy Thursday late afternoon, supine on the grass in the Cockpit of Hyde Park, alone and plunged in a torpor from which all efforts to arouse him had proved unsuccessful." (50) Echoes of Christ in Gethsemane are unmistakable here. In addition to this, Murphy's duties as night nurse in the Magdalen Mental Mercyseat require him to pass periodically through the stations of the cross.

At the height of his astrology craze, Murphy describes Mercury as "god of thieves, planet *par excellence* and mine," (31) and the characteristics of the mercurical type may be observed in him: wit, caution, subtlety, cunning, restlessness, worry, insomnia, and so on. This parallel is not minutely pursued from an historical point of view, however, and serves chiefly a unifying function on the aesthetic level.

Still another parallel to Murphy as a quester is the movement of the sun. Astrological correspondences will be more fully treated in the section on symbol and motif, but for the present we should observe that at the beginning of the book the sun is in Virgo, the Virgin. (Incidentally, this establishes an ironic counterpart to the relationship of Murphy and Celia.) When Murphy takes his job in the M.M.M. the sun has moved over into Libra, the Balance—his fate theoretically can still go either way. But on the day his ashes are dispersed throughout the public house, the sun moves into Scorpio, the House of Death. In the light of this evidence, metaphorical identification can be set up between Murphy and the sun or Apollo.

Murphy in motion can be seen then as related to Christ, Apollo, and Mercury. But in the stasis of his own mind he sees himself figured forth by Ixion and Tantalus, and visualizes eternal joy in the lee of Belacqua's rock and his embryonal repose, looking down at dawn across the reeds to the trembling of the austral sea and the sun obliquing to the north as it rose, immune from expiation until he should have dreamed it all through again, with the downright dreaming of an infant, from the spermarium to the crematorium. . . . He would have a long time lying there dreaming, watching the dayspring run through its zodiac, before the toil up hill to Paradise. (77-78)

Belacqua, a notoriously lazy Florentine lute-maker, is described by Dante as "*colui, che mostra sé più negligente,/che se pigrizia fosse sua sirocchia.*"[1] Admittedly such a destiny leaves a great deal to be desired. Nevertheless, for Murphy it represents a pleasant relief from the role of *pharmakos*, and an improvement on the eternal frustration of Ixion and Tantalus.

These are the closer archetypal kinsmen of Murphy. It should be observed that although such correspondences serve to identify him as a universal or typical man, their primary function remains the illumination of manner and theme. Only in these terms can we see how Murphy may be simultaneously Christ and Apollo and Mercury and Ixion and Tantalus and Belacqua—for each of his archetypes serves him in different situations. Thus in his relation to the world of material reality (the only world acknowledged by most of the other characters of the book) he sees himself as Tantalus or Ixion, yet in social intercourse with these same characters he occupies the position of the sun or Mercury, its nearest neighbor. In motion he is a *pharmakos* and in his conception of the quest deferred he is figured forth as Belacqua.

Murphy's archetypal values become significant as we see him moving through the plot of the book. When he is in stasis—that is, whenever he is not actively (or passively) engaged in his quest—he becomes little more than a puppet, and his body, like the bodies of the other characters, is described as a machine. One of his many static roles is that of financier, demonstrated when he defrauds the lunch counter of approximately .83 cups of tea:

The supreme moment in his degradations had come, the moment when, unaided and alone, he defrauded a vested interest. The sum involved was small, something between a penny and twopence (on the retail valuation). But then he had only fourpence worth of confidence to play with. . . . But no matter how the transaction were judged from the economic point of view, nothing could detract from its merit as a little triumph of tactics in the face of the most fearful odds. On the one hand a colossal league of plutomanic caterers, highly endowed with the ruthless cunning of the sane, having at their disposal all the most deadly weapons of the postwar recovery; on the other, a seedy solipsist and fourpence. (81-82)

For Murphy, the *plaisir de rompre* forms the rationale of social contacts, because people as such are barriers to his inner progress. "Murphy required for his pity no other butt than himself." (71) His love for Celia is primarily his body's love for her body; intellectually he remains undiverted from his goal. Pleasant as is the constant round of serenade, nocturne and aubade in Celia's bed, the joys of gratified desire are brief. In the end, "her efforts to make a man of him had made him more than ever Murphy." (190) But this should not imply that he does not know how to play the game; socially as well as financially Murphy is a manipulator. When a lover's quarrel is developing he thinks to himself: "What about a small outburst. It could do no harm, it might do good." (36) He also experiments with the simpler bodily pleasures. For example:

the sensation of the seat of a chair coming together with his drooping posteriors at last was so delicious that he rose at once and repeated the sit, lingeringly and with intense concentration. Murphy did not so often meet with these tendernesses that he could afford to treat them casually. The second sit, however, was a great disappointment. (80)

Similarly, laughter affords him only brief respite. On visualizing his triple pun—Why did the barmaid champagne? Because the stout porter bitter—

he staggered about on the floor . . . overcome by the toxins of this simple little joke. He sank down on the dream of Descartes linoleum, choking and writhing like a chicken with the gapes. . . . The fit was so much more like one of epilepsy than of laughter that Celia felt alarm. Watching him roll on the floor she . . . went to his assistance. . . . It was unnecessary, the fit was over, gloom took its place, as after a heavy night. (139-140)

Murphy observes human society but is not a part of it, and

in his mind a constant Cartesian struggle goes on between extension and thought. However, as the epigraph of Chapter IX indicates (*Il est difficile à celui qui vit hors du monde de ne pas rechercher les siens* [156]), Murphy cannot wholly dissociate himself from people: from society and its institutions, yes; but not from other questers of the dark. It is his hope that somewhere among the many closed systems of the patients at the M.M.M. he may find some sort of asocial companionship.

He would not have admitted that he needed a brotherhood. He did. In the presence of this issue (psychiatric-psychotic) between the life from which he had turned away and the life of which he had no experience . . . he could not fail to side with the latter. (176)

Murphy's quest is intimately involved with the search for non-Newtonian reality. Every cosmogeny describes the origin of the world in similar terms—"The earth was without form and void, and darkness was upon the face of the deep . . . and God separated the light from the darkness." Throughout history man has tried to further this divine work by imposing forms accessible to his intellect—language, art, the "laws" of nature and reason—on the chaos that surrounds him. Possibly history has shown a net gain for man, but this does not mean that chaos has diminished—if anything, its pressure only increases where it abuts on form. Unlike other members of his species, Murphy wants to return to the darkness: "It was not in order to obtain an obscene view of the surface that in days gone by the Great Auk dived under the ice, the Great Auk no longer seen above it." (193)

The philosophical distance between Murphy and his fellow-characters may be seen in the following passage. Miss Dew's dachshund, Nelly, has just snapped up Murphy's entire store of cookies.

Wylie in Murphy's place might have consoled himself with the thought that the Park was a closed system in which there could be no loss of appetite; Neary with the unction of an *Ipse dixit;* Ticklepenny with reprisal. But Murphy was inconsolable, the snuff of the dip stinking that the biscuits had lit in his mind, for Nelly to extinguish. (102)

Additional insight into the nature of Murphy's quest is also offered in the discourse on his mind:

Murphy's mind pictured itself as a large hollow sphere, hermetically closed to the universe without. This was not an impoverishment, for it excluded nothing that it did not itself contain. Nothing ever had been, was or would be in the universe outside it but was already present as virtual, or actual, or virtual rising into actual, or actual falling into virtual, in the universe inside it. . . . He distinguished between the actual and the virtual of his mind . . . as between that of which he had both mental and physical experience and that of which he had mental experience only. . . . The mind felt its actual part be above and bright, its virtual beneath and fading into dark, without however connecting this with the ethical yoyo. The mental experience was cut off from the physical experience, . . . the agreement of part of its content with physical fact did not confer worth on that part. . . . Thus Murphy felt himself split in two, a body and a mind. (107-109)

Murphy is trying to become a flawless microcosm,[2] and in the little world of the book he succeeds. But even though Murphy encompasses all the other characters and becomes paradoxically the moving nucleus of a motionless system, he is at the same time split in two. His problem is not, as Neary thinks, the reconciliation of the opposites; Murphy wants to make his mind master of his body, and as far as he is concerned, "any solution would do that did not clash with the feeling . . . that his mind was a closed system, subject to no principle of change but its own, self-sufficient and impermeable to the vicissitudes of the body." (109) At this stage Murphy is still trying to escape the fate of the Great Auk.

This division of mind and body, together with the three zones of consciousness, helps to explain the gulf separating Murphy's visual experience from his perception. During his alliance with Miss Counihan, Murphy had to close his eyes in order to see her. And in trying to summon up a vision of Celia,

it was as though some instinct had witheld her from accosting him in form until he should have obtained a clear view of her advantages, and warned her that before he could see it had to be

not merely dark, but his own dark. Murphy believed there was
no dark quite like his own dark. (90-91)

In contrast to this, Murphy's visual imagination is minutely
descriptive. After telling Celia his triple pun he pictures it
to himself in fine detail:

The barmaid, fresh from the country, a horse's head on a cow's
body, her crape bodice more a W than a V, her legs more an
X than an O, her eyes closed for the sweet pain, leaning out
through the hatch of the bar parlour. . . . The stout porter,
mounting the footrail, his canines gleaming behind a pad of
frothy whiskers. Then the nip, and Tintoretto's *Origin of the
Milky Way*. (140)

As the book opens, Murphy is momentarily at a stand-
still. His previous attempts to subordinate body to mind have
met with failure, and even his indispensible rocking-chair
offers only the negative value of an anodyne. He has tried
to escape into the church without success: his one suit, a
coppery-black relic of his days as a theology student, is
"entirely non-porus. It admitted no air from the outer world,
it allowed none of Murphy's own vapours to escape." (72)
Yet his mind remains free: "Murphy never wore a hat, the
memories it awoke of the caul were too poignant. . . ." (73)
The result of his association with the church is an ironic
inversion of its values. By his golden rule, "Murphy did no
more than as he would be done by," (21) and as he takes
his noonday tea at the lunch counter he delivers a silent grace:
"On this part of himself that I am about to indigest may the
Lord have mercy." (81) And evidently associating the church
with unrelieved bondage, "he would put in time walking
round and round Pentonville Prison. Even so at evening he
had walked round and round cathedrals that it was too
late to enter." (74) It is with some vague regret that Murphy
refuses to accept the panacea of religion, but there can be
no turning back from his journey into the dark.

Likewise, his most recent effort, Nearyan heart control, has
proved a fiasco:

For Murphy had such an irrational heart that no physician
could get to the root of it. Inspected, palpated, ausculated, per-
cussed, radiographed and cardiographed, it was all that a heart

should be. Buttoned up and left to perform, it was like Pe-
trouchka in his box. (3)

Nevertheless, he still has hope. When Celia first met him he
was standing in the mouth of Stadium Street, consulting al-
ternately the heavens and a starchart for June. And as she
soon realized, the way to Murphy is through the stars. For
this reason she has his "bull of incommunication" cast. And
when he later goes out to look for a job, the Nativity is his sole
comfort and amulet.

But astrology cannot provide the bliss Murphy dreams of.
For one thing, it is subject to external tampering. In Celia's
hands the stars sell out Murphy to the big world and tempt him
with the false idols of hearth and home. At this stage of
his development Murphy is still pursued by his personal
demons of knowledge and sex, and when the two join forces
against him, the effect is almost catastrophic. But not quite.
Murphy leaps at the first opportunity to escape Celia and the
macrocosm, and before his final plunge into the Boundless
he even transcends astrology.

The more his own system closed round him, the less he could
tolerate its being subordinated to any other. Between him and
his stars no doubt there was correspondence, but not in Suk's
sense. They were *his* stars, he was the prior system. He had
been projected, larval and dark, on the sky of that regrettable
hour as on a screen, magnified and clarified into his own
meaning. But it was *his* meaning. The moon in the Serpent was
no more than an image, a fragment of vitagraph. (182-183)

This rejection is only a part of Murphy's withdrawal from
the macrocosm. Although he seems to vacillate at times and
meander through occasional detours, his thematic movement
is unbroken. He has waded the bogs of institutionalism without mishap; he has hacked his way through the underbrush
of hedonism (Miss Counihan); he has shaken off the dust of
Neo-Pythagoreanism; and finally he overreaches the stars.
Evidence of this movement can be seen throughout the book:
although Murphy has been lured temporarily into a half-
hearted search for employment, he hisses rather than whistles
on his way, and as he regresses he notices a gradual narrowing
of the gap between body and mind, at times even an apparent

collusion between the two. This in turn leads him toward his final destination:

> Thus as his body set him free more and more in his mind, he took to spending less and less time in the light, spitting at the breakers of the world; and less in the half light, where the choice of bliss introduced an element of effort; and more and more and more in the dark, in the will-lessness, a mote in its absolute freedom. (113)

By the time Murphy reaches the M.M.M., the next-to-last station of his journey, he is at least partially prepared to accept its challenge:

> The issue therefore . . . lay between nothing less fundamental than the big world and the little world, decided by the patients in favour of the latter, revived by the psychiatrists on behalf of the former, in his own case unresolved. In fact, it was unresolved, only in fact. His vote was cast. "I am not of the big world, I am of the little world" was an old refrain with Murphy. . . . (178)

His position here does not seem altogether hopeless—*rapport* with the inmates of the M.M.M., categorically denied to the other staff members, may be extended to him. His superiors abuse him for his clumsiness in handling things, yet they are bound to acknowledge his skill in handling patients. But even though Murphy's mind may have chosen the microcosm, his body has its misgivings. The trailing ends of his former life still cling to him; the light and the half-light have not yet been fully extinguished by the dark. Murphy has dissociated himself from most of his possessions (books, pictures, postcards, musical scores and instruments) but is still dependent on his rocking-chair, "that aid to life in his mind from which he had never before been parted." (189) Nor can he fully erase the memory of Celia; he no longer thinks of her, "though he could sometimes remember having dreamt of her. If only he had been able to think of her, he would not have needed to dream of her." (189)

These are only minor problems, however, Pavlovian bells out of Murphy's past. Far more important is the challenge offered by the patients at the M.M.M. Here Murphy finds innumerable closed systems, many offering examples of the quest completed; yet near as he is to his goal spatially, he can-

not simply claim it without further ado. And as he takes the
night shift his situation becomes even more desperate:

By day he had not felt the gulf so painfully as he did now. . . .
There were the patients . . . circulating through the wards and
in the gardens. He could mix with them, touch them, speak
to them, watch them, imagine himself one of them. But in the
night of Skinner's there were none of these adminicles, no
loathing to love from, no kick from the world that was not his,
no illusion of caress from the world that might be. It was as
though the microcosmopolitans had locked him out. (239-240)

In fact things are so bad that Murphy even wonders if the
bliss of the microcosm may not be denied to those who crave
it even as to those who dread it.

When he enters the M.M.M. Murphy stakes everything.
Like the traditional quester who parlays his life into a kingdom, he puts up all his possessions and whatever peace of
mind he may have gained in previous pursuits (sex, philosophy, contemplation, etc.) against the contingency of winning
the little world here. And while his wager is in abeyance,
the fat is in the fire:

Nor did he succeed in coming alive in his mind any more. He
blamed this on his body, fussy with its fatigue after so much duty,
but it was rather due to the vicarious autology that he had been
enjoying since morning, in little Mr. Endon and all the other
proxies. That was why he felt happy in the wards and sorry
when the time came to leave them. He could not have it both
ways, not even the illusion of it. (189)

It is evident that Murphy needs help. Just as Dante
requires a Beatrice and Aeneas a sibyl, Murphy must have Mr.
Endon. Not that Mr. Endon volunteers to serve as his psy-
chopomp; he would be less Mr. Endon if he did. "The sad
truth was, that while Mr. Endon for Murphy was no less
than bliss, Murphy for Mr. Endon was no more than chess."
(242) Nevertheless, through association with the closed system
of this affable apnoeoid, Murphy is vouchsafed his first total
experience of the dark. At the end of their memorable chess
match,

Murphy began to see nothing. . . . His other senses found themselves at peace, an unexpected pleasure. Not the numb peace of

their own suspension, but the positive peace that comes when the somethings give way, or perhaps simply add up, to the Nothing. . . . Murphy with his head among the armies continued to suck in, through all the posterns of his withered soul, the accidentless One-and-Only, conveniently called Nothing. (246)

This marks the beginning of Murphy's end. One does not survive direct contact with Nothingness—but then, survival has never been Murphy's destiny. From this moment on, his final movement into the dark is accelerated and irrevocable. In a moment of communion with Mr. Endon's remarkable gaze, Murphy is granted a last mortal vision of the dark:

"the last at last seen of him
himself unseen by him
and of himself"

"The last Mr. Murphy saw of Mr. Endon was Mr. Murphy unseen by Mr. Endon. This was also the last Murphy saw of Murphy."

"The relation between Mr. Murphy and Mr. Endon could not have been better summed up than by the former's sorrow at seeing himself in the latter's immunity from seeing anything but himself."

"Mr. Murphy is a speck in Mr. Endon's unseen." (250)

It is now time for all the loose ends to be gathered up. Murphy leaves Mr. Endon and goes out into the starless night. Exit astrology. He sets out slowly for the nurses' quarters, taking off his clothes and discarding them on the way. Exit clerical insulation. Then,

when he was naked he lay down in a tuft of soaking tuffets and tried to get a picture of Celia. In vain. Of his mother. In vain. Of his father. . . . In vain. . . . He tried again with his father, his mother, Celia, Wylie, Neary, Cooper, Miss Dew, Miss Carridge, Nelly, the sheep, the chandlers, even Bom and Co., even Bim, even Ticklepenny and Miss Counihan, even Mr. Quigley. He tried with the men, women, children and animals that belong to even worse stories than this. In vain in all cases. He could not get a picture in his mind of any creature he had met, animal or human. (251-252)

Exit the world of forms. Murphy rises and goes to his garret and ties himself in his chair, vaguely intending to escape by returning to Brewery Road and Celia. But it is too late now— he has embarked on his journey:

He pushed off. . . . At one of the rock's dead points he saw, for a second, far beneath, the dip and radiator, gleam and grin; at the other the skylight, open to no stars. Slowly he felt better, astir in his mind, in the freedom of that light and dark that did not clash, nor alternate, nor fade nor lighten except to their communion. The rock got faster and faster, shorter and shorter, the gleam was gone, the grin was gone, the starlessness was gone, soon his body would be quiet. Most things under the moon got slower and slower and then stopped, a rock got faster and faster and then stopped. Soon his body would be quiet, soon he would be free.

The gas went on in the w.c., excellent gas, superfine chaos. Soon his body was quiet. (252-253)

Celia

As opposed to Murphy, Celia is described in precisely the police-blotter fashion: her introduction consists of an inventory of those physical circumferences which might be of special interest to a prospective client. Thus her age and instep are "unimportant," her head "small and round," but from neck to ankle her measurements are given to the nearest quarter inch. With these vital statistics entered, no further description of Celia is necessary; her appearance will be gauged by the impressions she makes on all the male characters of the book.

This means of introduction points up a number of interesting contrasts between Celia and Murphy. If the essence of Murphy is mind, the essence of Celia is body; if the character of Murphy is developed cumulatively and subjectively, Celia enters the action complete and detached as an obituary item; if Murphy moves through a cycle, Celia runs in circles. But all this does no more than point up the essential difference between "round" and "flat" characters—and as Beckett implies, Celia is one of the puppets. Nevertheless, if a finer distinction may be drawn, Celia seems to be an ellipsoid rather than a disc.

Like Murphy, Celia is not to be equated with any single

mythic predecessor; instead, she assumes several archetypal
identities in the course of her movement through the plot.
Yet since her thematic development is severely restricted in
comparison to Murphy's, we may expect to find her playing
somewhat fewer roles.

As her dimensions and name suggest, Celia may be identified as a heavenly goddess of love and fertility. Throughout
the book she has an aphrodisiac influence on all the male characters (excepting, of course, Ticklepenny and the brothers
Clinch), and like the foam-born Aphrodite she has a deep
affinity for the sea, but with a difference—when she first
met Murphy she was on the point of returning to it.

The dual nature of Aphrodite makes her a perfect archetype for Celia. In the role of Aphrodite Urania she is the
patroness of wedded love and fruitfulness, as Suk's chart
testifies, and in the vegetation myths she is the vessel of re-
birth who weeps in the autumn for her dead Adonis (Murphy). But as Aphrodite Pandemos she is, as her agnomen signifies, the goddess of all men—in other words, a whore. It is
hardly surprising that Murphy should see her as a "char-
Venus." (37)

But this mythic parallel should not be carried too far.
Since Celia exists dramatically only in relation to Murphy,
she must be regarded essentially as a foil. And for Murphy,
obsessed against his better judgment by the demands of his
body, all desirable young women are potential Aphrodites.

As an obstacle to his quest, Celia is seen by Murphy as a
Fury coming to carry him off, but this is not so much a metaphorical identification as the backlash of his sexual attraction
to her. In a similar vein she is also seen as a minor functionary
of an ironic Court of Love: "Yet it was not she, but Love,
that was the bailiff. She was but the bumbailiff." (27)

Celia then personifies the two faces of love. She offers the
pleasant round of serenade, nocturne, and aubade to Murphy's
body, but at the same time she detains him from his quest into
the dark. In this frame of reference Celia represents a kind of
half-light, moonlight. Since she is a woman, the moon is her
planet and it works on her behalf. Like the force of spring
tides Celia's power over Murphy increases as the moon approaches perigee. On the evening she persuades Murphy to

settle down and look for a job, "the moon, by a striking coincidence . . . was 29,000 miles nearer the earth than it had been for four years" and "exceptional tides were expected." (26) Conversely, on 11 October, the day when Murphy meets Ticklepenny and decides to leave Celia for the M.M.M., the moon is full again, but not nearly so near the earth as when last in opposition.

As we observe Celia in the dramatic structure of the book, the material elements of her character fall into place and form a significant pattern. Like most of the other characters she must "have" someone, but whereas Murphy endeavors to transcend his need for companionship and fails (he must have Mr. Endon), Celia deliberately orients her life toward the possession of another person. Her movement may be seen in terms of sexual relationships rotating from financial and universal (as Pandemos) through amorous and particular (as Urania), and back to the point of outset, forming a closed system. Forever needing someone, Celia must revolve eternally on the wheel of social supply and demand.

To Murphy, Celia is body and therefore the natural enemy of his mind. When she suggests that he go out to look for work, he sums up his dilemma laconically: "What have I now? . . . I distinguish. You, my body and my mind. . . . In the mercantile gehenna . . . to which your words invite me, one of these will go, or two, or all. If you, then you only; if my body, then you also; if my mind, then all." (39-40) But even if Murphy's mind is fully capable of defining and analyzing the danger Celia represents, his body still clings stubbornly to her. For this reason, her physical assets are a matter of primary importance. Niklaus Gessner points out in his stylistic examination of her introduction that "diese Darstellungsweise ist nicht nur leblos, sondern auch recht ausdrucksschwach," although "einige der Massangaben, wie z.B. 'Poitrine 90,0' und 'Tour de taille 67,0' können vom Leser in eine Vorstellung zurückübersetzt werden."[3] And these are precisely the measurements which are significant to Celia. To a certain extent she represents love, but beyond this she may be seen as a manifestation of pure body. For example, she establishes her liaison with Murphy by means of gesture. After having caught his eye, "for perhaps two minutes she

suffered this gladly, then with outstretched arms began slowly
to rotate. . . . When she came full circle she found, as she
had fully expected, the eyes of Murphy still open and upon
her." (14) And later when she learns that Murphy has been
to Brewery Road and left without waiting to see her, her
reaction is described in the same mechanical terms:

Celia went on slowly up the stairs. . . . The turn of the stair took
the body out of sight, but Miss Carridge could still see the hand
on the bannister, gripping, then sliding a little, gripping again,
then sliding a little more. (154-155)

A final key to the polarity of Celia and Murphy may be
observed in the differing ways they perceive the "dream
of Descartes" linoleum of their flat: "The vast floor area was
covered all over by a linoleum of exquisite design, a dim
geometry of blue, grey and brown that delighted Murphy
because it called Braque to his mind, and Celia because it delighted Murphy." (63)

Most of the characters in the book require that everything
remind them of something else. Only Celia, Mr. Endon, and
Murphy successfully manage to sever the bond between the
perceiver and the thing perceived. On her way to examine
the mortal remains of Murphy, "Celia leaning back with her
face to the window was aware only of all the colours of
light streaming back into the past and the seat thrusting forward," (256-257) while all the other people in the taxi with
her are busy evaluating the death of Murphy in terms of
personal advantage.

So far Celia seems quite two-dimensional. But through her
association with Murphy she temporarily follows in his footsteps. For a time she tries to recreate herself in an existen-
tialist manner, despite Murphy's essentialist rejoinders:

"I am what I do," said Celia.
"No," said Murphy. "You do what you are, you do a fraction
of what you are, you suffer a dreary ooze of your being into
doing." (37)

Eventually she realizes that Murphy is right, that she has
sentenced herself to walk the treadmill of being, "with the
swagger that could not be disguised." (150)

When Celia tries to enter into a new life with Murphy, she finds only darkness, and at this point we begin to see in her some kind of dramatic reversal or recognition. The new life turns out to be a double-edged weapon: if she has made him more than ever Murphy, he has made her less than ever Celia. Because of her need to possess Murphy, she begins to pursue him on his descending path. While he is ostensibly out seeking a job she spends most of the day in his rocking-chair:

She preferred sitting in the chair, steeping herself in these faint eddies [of light] till they made an amnion about her own disquiet, to walking the streets . . . or wandering in the Market, where the frenzied justification of life as an end to means threw light on Murphy's prediction, that livelihood would destroy one or two or all three of his life's goods. . . .
Thus in spite of herself she began to understand as soon as he gave up trying to explain. . . . She could not sit for long in the chair without the impulse stirring, tremulously, as for an exquisite depravity, to be naked and bound. (66-67)

And for a moment at least she is able, like Murphy, to come alive in her mind. When she moves upstairs into the old boy's room, she unpacks, strips off her clothing, and begins to rock herself out of the world of forms.

Now the silence above was a different silence, no longer strangled. The silence not of vacuum but of plenum, not of breath taken but of quiet air. The sky. She closed her eyes and was in her mind with Murphy, Mr. Kelly, clients, her parents, others, herself a girl, a child, an infant. In the cell of her mind, teasing the oakum of her history. Then it was finished, the days and places and things and people were untwisted and scattered, she was lying down, she had no history. (148-149)

Like Murphy Celia is drawn irresistably toward death, but unlike him she has a savior, the old boy upstairs who calls her back to humanity through his death. Here we encounter one of Beckett's open-end analogies. As a glance at the range of critical speculation about *En attendant Godot* will indicate, Beckett has not provided enough clues in the text of the play to establish any single positive metaphorical identification for Godot. As a result, bolder critics of the play have ventured to apply arbitrarily their own pet theories, and others have gone on an endless source hunt.[4] The figure of Godot has been suggested as an analogy for everything from God to *godichon* to a minor character in Balzac named Godeau who, like Godot, never shows up. Beckett himself says, "if I knew what Godot was, I would have said so."[5] In other words, Godot is what people wait for.

James Joyce has presented a universal man in the guise of HCE/Finn MacCool/Russian General/Napoleon/Persse O'Reilly, etc., by means of sheer verbal density, by packing into *Finnegans Wake* a mass of interfused identities. Beckett's technique, which becomes more consistent in his later works, is just the opposite of this: he supplies the reader with a hold vast enough to carry any analogical cargo, along with the vaguest sort of loading instructions, and leaves him to his task. Yet even though their methods differ, the results are similar. If Joyce's HCE is a plenum, Beckett's Godot is a vacuum; but the two approach one another as infinity approaches zero. They both succeed in creating the universal out of the particular.

But to return to the old boy upstairs: in the humanist sense he is anyone who dies, and his death diminishes Celia. Mythically he, like Murphy, may be seen as an ironic Christ— he has had two previous seizures, one on Shrove Tuesday and the other on Derby Day—yet as with Godot, these resemblances must not be pressed so far as to drive out universality. A dual vision of these characters should be maintained at all times, so as to blunt neither edge of the irony.

Celia has become accustomed to the sound of the old boy pacing the floor above her and, although she has never met him, she is inconsolable at his death. Murphy tries to comfort her, but "Celia was mourning, like all honest survivors, quite frankly for herself." (136) And when it is apparent that Murphy has left her for good, she moves upstairs into the room the old boy has vacated. In her own fashion Celia approaches the dark. She has died vicariously with the old boy, but her death is not consummated, and becomes a death in life. When Miss Carridge announces the arrival of Neary and company, Celia tells her "I have been so busy, so busy, so absorbed, my swan crossword you know, Miss

Carridge, seeking the rime, the panting syllable to rime with breath, that I have been dead to the voices of the street, dead and damned, Miss Carridge, the myriad voices." (229)

For a time it seems possible that Celia may be traveling in the same direction as Murphy, though by a different route. But her motion is negligible, for without Murphy she becomes nothing—that is to say, she reverts to her former existence. As she says, " 'When I think of what I was . . . who I was, what I am, and now dead, on a Sunday afternoon, with the sun singing, and the birds shining, to the voices of the STREET, then—' " (230) Finally, in a statement corresponding structurally to Murphy's "afflatulence," she delivers her manifesto of despair:

"At first I thought I had lost him because I could not take him as he was. Now I do not flatter myself."

"I was a piece out of him that he could not go on without, no matter what I did."

"He had to leave me to be what he was before he met me, only worse, or better, no matter what I did."

"I was the last exile."

"The last, if we are lucky." (234)

Unlike Murphy, who becomes one with the macrocosm in his death, Celia sinks back into the daily round: "So Neary and Celia cease slowly to need Murphy. He, that he may need her; she, that she may rest from need." (256) By the end of the book, the would-be butterfly is again a caterpillar.

Mr. Kelly

As Celia's *raison d'être* is Murphy, her paternal grandfather is a satellite in the Celian system. He appears only three times: the day Celia takes Murphy's Nativity to him (12 September); in Celia's imagination after she is certain Murphy has deserted her (7 October); and in the final scene of the book, when Celia has returned to her former life (26 October).

Since Mr. Kelly exists only in relation to Celia, no complex metaphorical parallels underlie his role, and it is quite

clear that he is to be seen as a puppet. After telephoning
Murphy, Celia makes her way to his flat in Tyburnia to
inform him of her recent alliance. On mention of Murphy's
name, "Mr. Kelly fell back in the bed, which closed his eyes,
as though he were a doll." (12) In order to be seen by him
Celia "set herself off in the line that his eyes must take on
their next declension and waited. When his head moved at
last, it was to fall with such abandon on his breast that he
caught and lost sight of her simultaneously." (13) Even his
moment of deepest bereavement, when Celia has left him for
Murphy, is recorded with flat, colorless precision: "The human eyelid is not teartight, the craters between nose and
cheekbone trapped the precious moisture, no other lachryma-
tory was necessary." (115)

Not only is Mr. Kelly a puppet—he is a thoroughly worn-
out puppet.

Mr. Kelly's face was narrow and profoundly seamed with a
life time of dingy, stingy repose. Just as all hope seemed lost it
burst into a fine bulb of skull, unobscured by hair. Yet a little
while and his brain-body ratio would have sunk to that of a
small bird. (11)

He does not look a day over ninety and by the end of the
book his evanescence is almost complete: "He wore his
kiting costume, a glistening slicker many sizes too large for
him and a yachting-cap many sizes too small, though the
smallest and largest of their kind obtainable." (276)

This does not mean that Mr. Kelly has won the Murphyan
battle of thought and extension, however: he is still firmly
attached to the putative desires of his rapidly atrophying body.
His perennial expletive is "My rump!" and his thoughts, when
not on kiting, turn invariably to lechery. When Celia comes
to ask his advice about Murphy, he has difficulty concen-
trating because "his attention was dispersed. Part was with
its caecum, which was wagging its tail; part was with his
extremities, which were dragging anchor. . . ." (19) And at
one point in the interview he even makes a tentative move
to establish a more than grand-paternal relationship with Celia:

"Approach, my child," said Mr. Kelly, slipping away a little
from his surroundings.

"Damn it, I am approached," said Celia. "Do you want me to get in beside you?" (24)

Not only is his body seen as a machine; his mind is described in the same terms. Celia comes to him for advice about Murphy because "she knew that if by any means she could insert the problem into that immense cerebrum, the solution would be returned as though by clockwork." (18) And so it is: like Murphy and Celia, Mr. Kelly also fires four Parthian shots:

"Chuck him."

"Sever your connexion with this Murphy . . . before it is too late."

"Terminate an intercourse that must prove fatal . . . while there is yet time."

"I bow to passion." (24-25)

Yet fine as the mechanism of Mr. Kelly's mind may be, like his body it is subjected to progressive disintegration. When Celia has left him, "his body seemed to spread over a vast area. . . . He found it hard to think, impossible to expand the sad pun . . . *Celia, s'il y a, Celia, s'il y a*, throbbing steadily behind his eyes." (115)

But despite the narrator's insistence that Mr. Kelly be regarded as a puppet, he is presented in rather fine detail. In a dramatic sense he is a sounding-board for Celia: in order to give the reader both a pre- and post-Murphyan view of her, Mr. Kelly plays the role of auditor, and to get inside Celia's mind when the outsiders (Neary, Wylie, Miss Counihan, and Cooper) confront her, he appears in spirit through the bars of her bedrail and sings the ephemeral nature of love. Beyond this mechanical function in the dramatic structure of the book, Mr. Kelly also plays a minor but significant thematic role as one of the many figures set in opposition to Murphy. On the levels of manner and matter this is readily apparent, but thematically it is perhaps less so. There are several clues to this antithetical relationship, but perhaps the most obvious is that signalled by the chairs. Both Murphy and Mr. Kelly have a great attachment for their chairs, Murphy for his rocker and Mr. Kelly for his self-propelled wheelchair. Yet paradoxically it is Murphy in his garret, bound to his chair by seven scarves, who is capable of significant movement; Mr. Kelly, rocketing through Kensington Gardens at speeds up to 12 m.p.h., remains thematically at rest. Like Celia he is incapable of change and turns deathlessly (and lifelessly) on the spit of habit. And the mechanism, like its owner, is running down—the levers of his wheelchair, which formerly worked like the pulls of a beer-engine, have by the end of the book decelerated to the pace of the tired heart.

This thematic parody of Murphy is also to be seen in Mr. Kelly's avocation, kiting. His kite is constantly in need of repair; each time we see Mr. Kelly before the final chapter he is mending it. However, in the closing pages of the book he finally achieves his goal and flies it out of sight. But like Murphy, who seeks the dark and finds oblivion, he too overshoots his mark:

Celia turned and looked at Mr. Kelly. He lay back sideways in the chair, his cheek on his shoulder, a fold of the slicker lifting his lips in a mild snarl, not dying but dozing. As she watched the winch sprang from his fingers, struck violently against the railing, the string snapped, the winch fell to the ground, Mr. Kelly awoke. (281)

The end of the kitestring skims across the water of the Round Pond and vanishes joyfully in the dusk, and the game is lost. Murphy wants to free his mind from his body and still retain his identity; Mr. Kelly wants to fly his kite to heaven and still hold on to the other end of the string. Both of them fail in succeeding. This suggests that the problem of Murphy's symbolic movement as a quester can be answered only by means of a paradox.

For a moment it seems that Mr. Kelly may follow Murphy to oblivion. As he wakes to see his kite has slipped its moorings, he

tottered to his feet, tossed up his arms high and wide and quavered away down the path that led to the water, a ghastly, lamentable figure. The slicker trailed along the ground, the skull gushed from under the cap like a dome from under its lantern, the ravaged

face was a cramp of bones, throttled sounds jostled in his throat.
(281-282)

And in a last desperate effort to regain his link with heaven,
Mr. Kelly actually sets himself in motion. But Celia stops
him in time and leads him back to his wheelchair, and he is
once more claimed by the world. Celia cannot have Mr.
Kelly when he is in pursuit of his kite, just as she cannot
have Murphy when he is in pursuit of the dark. As Murphy
dives into chaos, Mr. Kelly soars toward heaven—and Celia
is trapped on earth between them.

Mr. Kelly's pastime may be seen in still another frame of
reference. If Murphy's quest for the depths can be defined
as a regression, Mr. Kelly's kite flies in the opposite direction
thematically as well as physically, on the high road to God.
Therefore, as the kite climbs higher and higher, "the cord
wormed slowly off the winch—out, back a little, stop; out,
back a little, stop. The historical process of the hardened
optimists" until finally "Mr. Kelly let out a wild rush of line,
say the industrial revolution" and the kite reaches the end
of its tether. Meliorist to the end, Mr. Kelly feels his kitestring can measure the distance from the real to the ideal:
"Now he was in a position to determine the point at which
seen and unseen met." But we have learned through Murphy's
experience what this sort of illumination leads to. Mr. Kelly's
epiphany is "in no way inferior to that conferred (presum-
ably) on Mr. Adams by his beautiful deduction of Neptune
from Uranus." (279-280)

Then the string breaks.

Neary

At the center of those who search for Murphy stands Mr.
Neary. His entrance on the scene of action is quite dramatic:
standing in the Dublin General Post Office and contemplating
from behind the statue of Cuchulain,

Neary had bared his head, as though the holy ground meant
something to him. Suddenly he flung aside his hat, sprang forward, seized the dying hero by the thighs and began to dash
his head against his buttocks, such as they are. (42)

But he too is a Newtonian puppet. His sorrow is described in exactly the same manner as that of Mr. Kelly: "Neary closed his eyes. In vain. The human eyelid is not teartight (happily for the human eye)." (51) He joyfully acknowledges his need for other people: " 'As it is with the love of the body, so with the friendship of the mind, the full is only reached by admittance to the most retired places.' " (47) Even his voice has the ring of inauthenticity—"Neary began to speak, as it rather sounded, be spoken through" (215) —and like the other static figures of the book he too becomes little more than an object in the line of vision.

Mythically Neary calls to mind the archetype of the fisher-king, the unsuccessful quester doomed to impotence and immobility. Yet paradoxically it is he who seems best equipped for the quest. When Murphy sat at his feet and attempted vainly to achieve *apmonia* (the Pythagorean octave which unites the opposites), Neary appeared to possess admirable control:

This man, at that time, could stop his heart more or less whenever he liked and keep it stopped, within reasonable limits, for as long as he liked. This rare faculty . . . he exercised frugally, reserving it for situations irksome beyond endurance, as when he wanted a drink and could not get one, or fell among Gaels and could not escape, or felt the pangs of hopeless sexual inclination. (3)

Neary has studied with the monks north of the Nerbudda; he has learned the principles of *apmonia* from Pythagoras and *isonomy* from Alkmaion; he is familiar with Aristotle's figure of the three lives (theoretic, practical, and apolaustic), yet he remains immobile. While his former pupil gradually moves beyond society and into the dark, Neary remains at the beck and call of Miss Counihan; while Murphy considers the relation kick-kicker as a starting point in the actual and proceeds from there through the virtual into the ideal, where neither kick nor caress exists, Neary employs the metaphor only to sum up his rationale of social intercourse:

He thought of his latest *voltefesses*, at once so pleasant and so painful. Pleasant, in that Miss Counihan had been eased; painful, in that Murphy had been made worse; *fesses*, as being the part best qualified by nature not only to be kicked but also to mock the kicker, a paradox strikingly illustrated by Socrates, when he turned up the tail of his abolla at the trees. (200)

All his knowledge degenerates to such ends. When Murphy left him, Neary's tetrakyt[6] was Miss Dwyer:

"Murphy, all life is figure and ground."
"But a wandering to find home," said Murphy.
"The face," said Neary, "or system of faces, against the big blooming buzzing confusion. I think of Miss Dwyer." (4)

And now it is Miss Counihan: "Neary besieged Miss Counihan with attention, sending her mangoes, orchids, Cuban cigarettes and a passionately autographed copy of his tractate, *The Doctrine of the Limit*." (50) When his heart is not in suspension it pants after her. Unlike Murphy, who finally manages to escape Celia, Neary is only too happy to compromise his knowledge in the proximity of Miss Counihan.

Aesthetically Neary occupies the center of the second epicycle surrounding Murphy, and within his own system he motivates the actions of his satellites, Miss Counihan and Wylie; but thematically he closely resembles Mr. Kelly. Their relationship is that of two lesser magnitudes to a third, Murphy. Neary's movement (which is dramatic rather than thematic) may be seen as an inverted parody of Murphy's, for it consists of a perpetual endeavor to make the mind a willing servant of the body. To this end he has experimented with *apmonia* and *isonomy*, pseudo-orientalism, "huddled in the tod of his troubles like an owl in ivy, inundating with green tea a bellyful of bird's-nest soup, chop suey, noodles, sharks' fins and ly-chee syrup," (115-116) pseudo-Hellenism with his feet crossed on a hot water bag: "for it tickled his smattering of Greek urns, where Sleep was figured with crossed feet," (207) and he is relentlessly drawn toward the repudiation of the known—all without success. For bound as he is to sensual desire, each amorous misadventure is to him another death, and death of the body is his greatest fear. When Miss Counihan leaves with Wylie,

a curious feeling had come over Neary, namely that he would not get through the night. He had felt this before, but never

quite so strongly. In particular he felt that to move a muscle or
utter a syllable would certainly prove fatal. He breathed with
heavy caution through the long hours of darkness, trembled
uncontrollably and clutched the chair-arms. He did not feel cold,
far from it, nor unwell, nor in pain; he simply had this alarming
conviction that every second was going to announce itself the first
of his last ten minutes or a quarter of an hour on earth. (224)

Wylie and Miss Counihan

Wylie and Miss Counihan met face to face, a trying experience
for them both.
"You cur," said Miss Counihan, getting her blow in first.
"You bitch," said Wylie.
They belonged to the same great group. (210)

Even though individually each of them forms the center
of a self-motivated universe, Wylie and Miss Counihan may
be considered as a pair rather than singly, for, along with
Cooper, they compose the system oriented around Neary.
Therefore, since they stand twice removed from Murphy, it
is not surprising that they should be figured forth as simple
and unvarying "flat" characters.

Needle Wylie appears on the scene in the nick of time
to rescue Neary in the General Post Office, and immediately
the design of his character is revealed: small and thin and
sharp-featured, Wylie is, as his name suggests, an opportunist
par excellence. Social machination is his *forte* and lechery
his sport. His immediate goals are money (which Neary has)
and Miss Counihan (whom Neary would like to have), and
all his actions throughout the book are directed toward the
acquisition and enjoyment of these. Even his moments of
relatively abstract speculation are sullied with self-interest.

The distinction between Cartesian Murphy and Newtonian
Wylie may be observed in the nature and quality of their
perception:

His [Wylie's] way of looking was as different from Murphy's
as a *voyeur's* from a *voyant's*, though Wylie was no more the
one in the indecent sense than Murphy was the other in the
supradecent sense. The terms are only taken to distinguish
between the vision that depends on light, object, viewpoint, etc.,
and the vision that all those things embarrass. (90)

Miss Counihan also is wholly concerned with her physical well-being. Like Wylie she has the gift of non-introspection: "Miss Counihan could think ill of her partners, past, present and prospective, without prejudice to herself. This is a faculty that no young man or woman, stepping down into the sexpit, should be without." (255) And she too is adept in the art of social manipulation; after brushing Neary aside she picks him up again with ease by bumping into him skillfully in the Mall, and she assures Neary's continued generosity by keeping him at his wits' end:

A feature of Miss Counihan's attitude to Neary had been the regularity of its alternation. Having shown herself cruel, kind, cruel and kind in turn, she could no more welcome his arrival at her hotel than green, yellow, green is a legitimate sequence of traffic lights. (55)

Although she regards herself as a grass Dido, in a sense she may be thought of as a parody of Celia, in that she habitually plays Venus to every man's Adonis:

She would not identify herself more closely with Wylie than was convenient to her purpose (Murphy) or agreeable to her appetite. If she treated him with less rigour than she had Neary, it was simply because the latter took away her appetite. But she had made it clear to the one as she had to the other, that so long as any hope of Murphy remained her affections were to be regarded as in a state of suspension. (126)

Like Wylie she is in pursuit of wealth and those who have it. She is delighted to hear that Murphy has gone to London, the "Mecca of every young aspirant to fiscal distinction," (53) where "such a nice young man, who for all she knew to the contrary was steadily amassing a large fortune so that she might not be without any of the little luxuries to which she was accustomed, and whom of course she loved very dearly." (53)

As the narrator observes, "she was just like any other beautiful Irish girl, except, as noted, more markedly anthropoid," (118) but Miss Counihan has physical resources which immediately endear her to both Neary and Wylie. Wylie has long been her worshipper from afar, through binoculars. As he tells Neary, "'What a bust! . . . All centre

and no circumference!' " (60) And throughout the book Miss
Counihan uses her body with paralyzing effect; when Wylie
and Neary outdistance her in a contest of wits,

Miss Counihan rose, gathered her things together, walked to the
door and unlocked it with the key that she exiled for that purpose
from her bosom. Standing in profile against the blazing corridor,
with her high buttocks and her low breasts, she looked not
merely queenly, but on for anything. And these impressions
she enhanced by simply advancing one foot a pace, settling all
her weight on the other, inclining her bust no more than was
necessary to preserve her from falling down backwards and
placing her hands upon her moons, plump and plain. (219-220)

Against such tactics Wylie would seem to have little chance.
But he soon realizes Miss Counihan's charms are also her
most vulnerable points:

A man could no more work a woman out of position on her
own ground of sentimental lech than he could outsmell a dog.
Her instinct was a menstruum, resolving every move he made,
immediately and without effort, into its final implications for her
vanity and interest. The only points at which Miss Counihan was
vulnerable were her erogenous zones and her need for Murphy.
(126-127)

Wylie is moderately successful with Miss Counihan, for he
is a past master of the leching game. "A kiss from Wylie
was like a breve tied, in long slow amorous phrase, over bars'
times its equivalent in demi-semiquavers. Miss Counihan had
never enjoyed anything quite so much as this slow-motion
osmosis of love's spittle." (117-118) Later, to dispel Miss
Counihan's tears, Wylie applies with great artistry the
"astringent kiss, with a movement like a barber's clippers."
(124)

Although Miss Counihan and Wylie both personify the
stasis dictated by the body and its daily round of desires,
they do make occasional efforts to reach a higher plane of
existence. Yet no matter how much they engage in the
Murphyan game of gnostic repartee, neither can escape the
level of self-gratification. For example:

[Miss C.:]   There is a mind and there is a body—
[Neary:]   Shame! Kick her arse! Throw her out!

[Wylie:]	On the one parched palm, the swelling heart, the dwindling liver, the foaming spleen, two lungs with luck, with care two kidneys, and so on.
[Neary:]	And so forth.
[Wylie:]	And on the other, the little ego and the big id.
[Neary:]	Infinite riches in a w.c.
[Miss C.:]	This ineffable counterpoint, this mutual comment, this sole redeeming feature . . .
[Wylie:]	She quite forgets how it goes on, she will have to go right back to the beginning, like Darwin's caterpillar.
[Neary:]	Perhaps Murphy did not take her any further.
[Miss C.:]	Everywhere I find defiled in the crass and unharmonious unison, the mind at the cart-tail of the body, the body at the chariot-wheels of the mind. I name no names. (218)

All these characters are hopelessly trapped. In the beginning of the book Wylie is attracted to Miss Counihan; but once in London his interest wanes, and when he meets Celia the wheel begins its second revolution. Similarly, Miss Counihan plays an endless (and fruitless) game of self-betterment. Her affair with Murphy has fallen through; Wylie deserts her; and at the end of the book Neary, learning that he is free to roam London with impunity, "passed her rapidly at a comfortable remove, his hat raised in salute and his head averted. Miss Counihan followed slowly." (273)

Beyond instinct Miss Counihan knows only what she has learned verbatim from Murphy, and Wylie's *Weltanschauung*, although it appears in various forms, may be reduced to the dictum: "'The syndrome known as life is too diffuse to admit of palliation. For every symptom that is eased, another is made worse. The horse leech's daughter is a closed system. Her quantum of wantum cannot vary.'" (57)[7]

Stasis is the cornerstone of Wylie's philosophy. Murphy is incessantly in motion, but Wylie (and Neary, under Wylie's influence) clings stubbornly to his arid existence. Miss Counihan establishes a stasis by seeing herself as an immutable plenum; Wylie does it in terms of Newton's Third Law of Motion:

"Humanity is a well with two buckets," said Wylie, "one

going down to be filled, the other coming up to be emptied."
    "What I make on the swings of Miss Counihan," said Neary,
"if I understand you, I lose on the roundabouts of the non-Miss
Counihan."
    "Very prettily put," said Wylie. (58-59)

    Thus Wylie and Miss Counihan (like Celia, Mr. Kelly,
and Neary) represent alternatives to the quest. But thematically as well as aesthetically, they stand twice removed from
Murphy, in that they are not even aware of the existence
of his motion, and to each of them Murphy is a means and
not an end. To Celia he is a potential husband, to Neary, a
potential friend; but to Miss Counihan he stands for sexual
and economic gratification, and to Wylie, he is a bridge to be
crossed on the way to Miss Counihan.

Cooper

    Instrumental to the Nearyan system is Cooper, *âme
damnée* and man-of-all-work. His name—from the Dutch
kooper, a floating grogshop—is particularly appropriate. Although he is apparently one stage further removed from
Murphy than the members of the system (he seeks Murphy
only at the command of Neary, Wylie, and Miss Counihan),
within the group he serves a unifying function, operating in
fact as a triple-agent. Historically Cooper may be seen as an
ironic version of the stock comic figure of the wily slave, a
type represented by such diverse characters as Ariel in *The
Tempest* and Jeeves in the P. G. Wodehouse novels. As such
he serves a necessary purpose in plot development and acts as
a foil for the revelation of character.
    But in addition to this rather commonplace dramatic
function, Cooper occasionally seems to reveal an unsuspected
dimension of character. The thumbnail sketch given in his
entrance strikes a familiar chord:

Cooper's only visible humane characteristic was a morbid crav-
ing for alcoholic depressant. So long as he could be kept off the
bottle he was an invaluable servant. He was a low-sized, clean-
shaven, grey-faced, one-eyed man, triorchous, and a non-smoker.
He had a curious hunted walk, like that of a destitute diabetic in

a strange city. He never sat down and never took off his hat. (54)

When we finally learn that he walks with a crutch, the likeness becomes unmistakable. Cooper is a prototype for the later Beckett hero, Watt/Molloy/Malone/Unnamable, and in terms of the later works, Murphy's end is his beginning. The Beckettian progression appears occasionally: while Miss Counihan (static) is an omnivorous reader and Murphy (transitional) a strict non-reader, Cooper is an analphabete. Similarly, while love to Miss Counihan signifies the high road to fortune and to Murphy the subjugation of mind to body, love for Cooper has already descended to the Molloy level:

the only two good angels [the Engels sisters?] he had ever been able to care for, simultaneously as ill luck would have it, the one, a Miss A, then a brunette, was now in her seventeenth year of His Majesty's pleasure, while the other, a Miss B, also formerly a brunette, had not yet succumbed to her injuries. (206)[8]

But there is still another dimension to Cooper. For some reason, he is unable to sit or remove his hat. "It was true that Cooper never sat, his acathisia was deep-seated and of long standing. It was indifferent to him whether he stood or lay, but sit he could not." (119) His goal throughout the book is to sit; this small pleasure, of such infinite satisfaction to Murphy, is denied him. Then, suddenly, when Murphy dies, Cooper sits.

Cooper did not know what had happened to set him free of those feelings that for so many years had forbidden him to take a seat or uncover his head, nor did he pause to inquire. He placed his ancient bowler crown upward on the step, squatted high above it, set his teeth, flung his feet forward into space and came down on his buttocks with the force of a pile ram. (273)

Here it is apparent that Cooper's thematic function extends beyond that of the wily slave. Is he a messenger like Moran, commissioned to hound Murphy without rest until he dives beneath the surface, is he then a quadruple-agent? At any rate, Cooper finally gets his man and unites him ironically with the universe.

Mr. Endon

Murphy's "tab" at the M.M.M. is a paragon of the closed system. As his name indicates (from the Greek *endo*, within) he is completely sealed off from the outside world. A debonair, imperial figure in his fine dressing-gown of scarlet byssus faced with black braid, black silk pajamas and purple poulaines, to Murphy he is a fitting representative of the microcosm. He is totally self-sufficient, even in his chosen manner of suicide, asphyxia, which makes use of no external aids; and the unruffled calm of his existence makes Murphy his humble and emulous admirer.

The languor in which he passed his days, while deepening every now and then to the extent of some charming suspension of gesture, was never so profound as to inhibit all movement. His inner voice did not harangue him, it was unobtrusive and melodious, a gentle continuo in the whole consort of his hallucination. The bizarrerie of his attitudes never exceeded a stress laid on their grace. In short, a psychosis so limpid and imperturbable that Murphy felt drawn to it as Narcissus to his fountain. (186)

But, as expected, there is a hair in the soup of Murphy's affection for Mr. Endon. Murphy has come to the M.M.M. in order to study the techniques of cultivating the bodytight mind, but he does not realize that one cannot have his microcosm and share it too. This he learns through the chessy eye of Mr. Endon: "Mr. Endon would have been less than Mr. Endon if he had known what it was to have a friend; and Murphy more than Murphy if he had not hoped against his better judgment that his feeling for Mr. Endon was in some small degree reciprocated." (241)

If Mr. Endon is to be approached at all, he must be approached through his one pastime, chess. But at the end of a particularly rewarding game, as Murphy begins to feel he is making real progress, having experienced the rare treat of Nothingness, he sees himself in Mr. Endon's eyes:

In shape they were remarkable, being both deep-set and pro-
tuberant, one of Nature's jokes involving sockets so widely
splayed that Mr. Endon's brows and cheekbones seemed to have
subsided. And in colour scarcely less so, having almost none.
For the whites, of which a sliver appeared below the upper
lid, were very large indeed and the pupils prodigiously dilated,
as though by permanent excess of light. The iris was reduced
to a thin glaucous rim of spawnlike consistency. . . . All four
lids were overted in an octropion of great expressiveness, a
mixture of cunning, depravity and rapt attention. Approaching
his eyes still nearer Murphy could see the red frills of mucus, a
large point of suppuration at the roots of an upper lash, the
filigree of veins like the Lord's Prayer on a toenail and in the
cornea, horribly reduced, obscured, and distorted, his own
image. (248-249)

Brought face to face with this preview of himself in the oblivion of Mr. Endon's sightless gaze, Murphy realizes he has
come too far. He hurries to his rocker in search of solace
and resolves to return to society and Celia—but it is too late
now, the world of forms can never return.

Rosie Dew

During Murphy's noonday idyll near the Cockpit in Hyde
Park he is accosted by an extremely low and long dachshund
bitch and her mistress, a middle-aged spiritual medium named
Rosie Dew. Miss Dew engages him to mind her pet while she
attempts to feed two heads of lettuce to a nearby flock of
sheep, but in her absence the dachshund eats Murphy's entire
store of provisions. Miss Dew returns and compensates his
loss with three pence, then leaves the park and goes home to
attempt to evoke the spirit of her benefactor's father.
    Seen dramatically, Rosie Dew's appearance is wholly
superfluous. She neither participates in the action of the book
nor provides a transitional interlude, for after her brief scene
the narration returns immediately to Murphy, still in the park.
Her presence therefore must be justified on thematic grounds.
Like the other minor characters (Miss Counihan in particular)
Rosie Dew is a marked physical type; she suffers from an
advanced case of duck's disease.

Duck's disease is a distressing pathological condition in which
the thighs are suppressed and the buttocks spring directly from
behind the knees, aptly described in Steiss's nosonomy as Panpygoptosis. (97)

With regard to this affliction Miss Dew may be seen as a
reverse image of Miss Counihan, and where the latter tends
to be physically attractive, the former invariably repels. Rejected by her own species as an unlovable object, she turns
to animals for affection, but even they are revolted by her.
The sheep in the park may be a dingy, undersized, misshapen
lot, yet "they turned their broody heads aside from the
emetic" (100) and she is forced to stray further afield in her
search for love.

Like all ill-starred questers, Miss Dew must admit defeat.
Her offering of love is summarily rejected; the sheep will not
eat her lettuce either in her presence or out of it. She leaves
the park, "her lettuce turned down, her mortification, her pet
and herself in her pet insulted, the threepence gone that she
had earmarked for a glass of milk." (103) And the only thing
in store for her is a symbolic aggravation of her deformity
in the form of a boot, sent to her by her maleficent benefactor,
Lord Gall of Wormwood.

Nevertheless Miss Dew, as her name suggests, is a hard-
core optimist. Her control, a panpygoptotic Manichee of the
fourth century named Lena,

had not, according to her own account, been raised so wholly a
spiritual body as yet to sit down with much more comfort than
she had in the natural. But she declared that every century
brought a marked improvement and urged Miss Dew to be
of good courage. In a thousand years she might look forward
to having thighs like anyone else, and not merely thighs, but
thighs celestial. (104)

So, Blavatskyan optimism notwithstanding, Miss Dew's
immediate prospects are none too rosy. She and Nelly are
seen once more after this, in the final chapter of the book, and
things look as dim as ever for them. Another present is waiting from Lord Gall, accompanied by the message: " 'If this
pair of socks does not prove more productive, I shall have
to try a new control.' " (278)

A curious similarity may be noted in Rosie Dew and Cooper. For reasons psychic and somatic, both have difficulty in sitting, and both may possibly be messengers of the dark. Yet Cooper is capable of limited change, while Miss Dew apparently is not. Unable to sit at all until Murphy's death, Cooper does finally manage to perform the act. On the other hand, Miss Dew is able to sit, but on good authority she cannot hope to sit with comfort in less than a millenium. At any rate, both seem to be well removed from the promised land.

Miss Carridge

Like Rosie Dew and Cooper, Miss Carridge is more caricature than character. Drawn with a single stroke, she is notable only for her monumental hogo. Despite the application of shaving soap, scent, toilet soap, foot salts, bath cubes, dentifrices, deodorants, and even depilatories, she remains a victim of the "tragic quality, that which the Romans called *caper*." (134) Aside from this remarkable trait there is little to distinguish her from the other puppets. Like Miss Counihan she is an avid reader: the Bible is her strength and "A.E." her weakness. Her favorite epithet—"My rump!"—recalls Mr. Kelly, and like Wylie and Miss Counihan her principal sin is venality. When the old boy upstairs commits suicide, Miss Carridge reflects that she

was not a penny out of pocket, not one penny. The police, not she, had called the doctor, therefore his fee was on them. The bloody dilapidation of her lovely lino was amply covered by the month's advance rent paid by the old boy the day before. She had carried off the whole affair in splendid style. (136)

In fact she refuses to believe the old boy really committed suicide, since he had paid his rent in advance.

As Rosie Dew waddles like a duck, Miss Carridge's bodily movements are also barely anthropoidal. On finding the old boy dead, "she came speeding down the stairs one step at a time, her feet going so fast she seemed on little caterpillar wheels" and then "capered about in the street like a consternated ostrich." (135)

In the dramatic structure of the book Miss Carridge, like Mr. Kelly, is a supporting player for Celia. She appears only in relation to Celia and serves as her foil during Murphy's absence at the M.M.M. As Celia begins to move slowly toward the dark, Miss Carridge opposes her like an *eiron* from the world of forms: for this reason her reactions are conventional to a fault. As she runs out into the street to inform a policeman of the death of the old boy, "her mind was so collected that she saw clearly the impropriety of letting it appear so," (135) and later, in recounting the event to Celia, she tries to make his suicide appear an accident.

Thematically Miss Carridge is another of the puppets from the world of extension. But her relation to Celia may also be a reminder of the perils of the dark. Like a spirit from the nether world she habitually appears before Celia bearing a cup of Lapsang Souchong (note the bilingual ambiguity), with ominous admonitions to "drink it before it coagulates" (68) and "drink it before it curdles." (133) Similarly, as her name ironically implies, she plays a quasi-maternal role towards Celia, waiting on her and assuring her that Murphy had wished to see her during his sortie from the M.M.M. to Brewery Road. Apparently Celia is the only person who has ever received a cup of Lapsang Souchong *gratis* from the penurious hand of Miss Carridge.

Austin Ticklepenny

Another puppet, Ticklepenny—"Gussy" to his intimates, of whom Murphy is not one—is introduced frankly as a piece of plot-machinery:

This creature does not merit any particular description. The merest pawn in the game between Murphy and his stars, he makes his little move, engages an issue and is swept from the board. Further use may conceivably be found for Austin Ticklepenny in a child's halma or a book-reviewer's snakes and ladders, but his chess days are over. (84-85)

Dramatically he serves as the link between Murphy and the M.M.M. Along with the brothers Clinch, he is the representative of the big world impinging on the little. Therefore he may be seen to play the same sort of role for Murphy as that which Miss Carridge plays for Celia. Murphy gains admittance to the *sanctum sanctorum* of the M.M.M. because of Ticklepenny's desire to escape from it. Ticklepenny, a male nurse torn between the Charybdis of the microcosm and the Scylla of quitting his job unpaid, provides Murphy with a wedge into the little world by arranging for Murphy to assume his duties.

Like many of the other minor figures of the book, Ticklepenny is a garden-variety comic Irishman. Self-billed as Dublin's Pot Poet, he calls to mind an evening at the Cheshire Cheese adapted for vaudeville. The description of his verse reeks of the Irish Renaissance; his pentameters are

as free as a canary in the fifth foot (a cruel sacrifice, for Ticklepenny hiccuped in end rimes) and at the caesura as hard and fast as his own divine flatus and otherwise bulging with as many minor beauties from the gaelic prosodoturfy as could be sucked out of a mug of Beamish's porter. (88-89)

By profession a retired poet and by necessity a practicing potboy, Ticklepenny incarnates the ironic view of the artist. His pint-pentameter ratio having got out of hand, he has consulted a Dublin physician of German descent who advised him to " 'giff de pooze ub or go kaputt' " and gave him a "shit" (88) (N.B.: one point for Beckett in the author-censor game) to the M.M.M. for a mild course in dipsopathic discipline.

Throughout his interview with Murphy he makes hopeful homosexual "genustuprations," but "Murphy had such an enormous contempt for rape that he found it no trouble to go quite limp at the first sign of its application." Even in his avocation Ticklepenny is a failure.

With regard to theme Ticklepenny represents the same sort of glib superficiality as Neary. After pushing his business card into Murphy's line of sight, he explains: " 'When I failed to gain your attention . . . by means of what the divine son of Ariston calls the vocal stream issuing from the soul through the lips, I took the liberty as you notice.' " (85) And like Neary he is addicted to the repudiation of the visible: "Ticklepenny was immeasurably inferior to Neary in every way, but they had certain points of contrast with Murphy in common. One was this pretentious fear of going mad. Another was the inability to look on, no matter what the spectacle." (89) Inadvertently he becomes the instrument of Murphy's death. In connecting a jury-rig extension for Murphy's gas radiator, he gives him the next-to-last shove toward chaos, the last being administered by Mr. Endon's gaze of cosmic indifference. And in a clandestine visit to the garret shortly before Murphy's death, he affords a last glimpse of the big world in opposition to the small. Murphy wakes from a session in his rocker to find Ticklepenny beside him. Ticklepenny warns him that he is developing the look of Clarke, who has been in a catatonic stupor the last three weeks, repeating for hours on end the phrase: " 'Mr. Endon is *very* superior.' " (193) Murphy's gratified look on hearing this comparison so alarms Ticklepenny that he feels compelled to caution him of the dangers of the dark, in characteristic fashion:

"You want to mind your health," said Ticklepenny.
"In what way did I remind you of Clarke?" said Murphy.
"You want to take a pull on yourself," said Ticklepenny. "Good night." (194)

CHAPTER III

Symbol and Motif

DESPITE its tight organization and verbal economy, *Murphy* is not essentially a symbolic work, in the modern sense of the term; that is to say, its themes are not developed chiefly by means of analogy, but through the ironic narrational focus associated with Menippean satire. This does not mean however that the book relies solely on the resources of descriptive language—the distinction to be made is one of degree rather than of kind. The burden of meaning may be sustained by the narrator, but it is also reinforced and given aesthetic shape by auxiliary structures of symbol and motif.

Since these terms have blackened so much paper as to be almost meaningless without qualification, *symbol* will designate here, as its etymology suggests, a throwing-together or spatial patterning, and *motif* its counterpart in time. Observed together in the narrative they become one, but separated out, symbol may be seen as motif in stasis, and motif symbol in action. As components of the predicaments to be discussed, symbol is chiefly a function of matter and theme, motif of manner.

Light/Dark Symbolism

Throughout the book the principle of contending opposites is objectified by means of light/dark symbolism. Murphy's movement through the plot is a movement from light into darkness, and even as the book opens he is well on his way: "The corner in which he sat was curtained off from the sun." (1) As he works his chair up to its maximum rock he temporarily moves out of the big world of accident where the light never wanes the same way twice, but his

65

rocking-chair affords only a brief reconciliation of the opposites. As long as Murphy's body is bound and out of
contention, his mind is able to regard the light and dark in a
harmonious balance, but as soon as his physical needs become involved, the scales are tipped against him. Even the
loss of his cookies to a passing dog can extinguish the *ignis
fatuus* generated by his appetites. By the time he reaches his
last station, the M.M.M., he is more accustomed to the dark
and less susceptible to entreaties from the light. Even his
skylight, opening out on a starless heaven, helps him overcome his dependence on astrology. But despite this regression
he still must have a token amount of light; when he retires
to his garret he invariably lights a candle. Finally, after the
chess game with Mr. Endon, the light is extinguished and
Murphy drifts into total darkness. As he tries to rock himself
into the old sense of the communion of light and dark, the last
remaining light, the glow of the gas heater, goes out.

Thus his movement into the dark is complete. Yet one
thing is especially significant here: the final movement is
not of Murphy's making. Up to a point he has controlled his
chiaroscuro: the dark has always been *his* dark, and only
one of the three mental zones at his disposal. But only up
to a point.

As Samuel Mintz has observed, the influence of the Cartesian philosopher Geulincx can be seen here.[1] Murphy reflects Cartesian dualism, in that his inner schism of extension
and thought is paralleled symbolically by the opposition of
light and dark. But why three zones? Why a trichotomy
instead of a dichotomy?

The celebrated dream of Descartes may help to explain
the zoning of Murphy's mind and its relation to the light and
dark. His first zone corresponds to the sensation of intellectual
clarity described by Descartes before the dream: "Dans le
chaos obscur de cette science [la géométrie] . . . j'ai aperçu
je ne sais quelle lumière à laquelle les plus épaisses ténèbres
pourront se dissiper." It is this light which enables him to
"pénétrer jusqu'au coeur du royaume de la science."[2] But then
comes the dream sequence of 10 November 1619: the Prome-
thean blaze wanes in a zone of half-light sliding toward darkness, where

il n'y a plus seulement un dédoublement de l'être, mais une multiplication infinie de celui-ci en d'innombrables personnalités éphémères qui ont de moins en moins rapport entre elles. Alors le temps lui-méme se fragment. Il n'y a plus que des instants affectifs, chacun éprouvé pour lui seul et vécu isolément.[3]

Two hours later, in the second dream the *deus ex machina* enters in and

la gráce transcende le présent, elle en fait un moment d'illumination infiniment simple, de lumière pure, dont le rayonnement subsiste encore après qu'elle a disparu: "En ayant ouvert les yeux, il aperçut beaucoup d'étincelles de feu répandues par la chambre."[4]

And in the final dream an epiphany of universal harmony is attained, symbolized by a dictionary, a series of portraits, and a collection of poems.

Superficially this bears little resemblance to Murphy's zones. However, it must be kept in mind that Murphy is not Descartes' *Doppelgänger*—at most he may experience the ironic side of the Cartesian equation, in which all signs have been changed. It is reasonable to assume that Murphy has sought knowledge in the light (after all, he has studied with Neary), but as he comes free in his mind the zones of half-light and dark take on increased significance and offer him more and more pleasure. His movement is thus opposed to that of Descartes; the darker zones which occasion anguish and terror in Descartes become for Murphy infinitely desirable:

It was pleasant to lie dreaming on the shelf beside Belacqua, watching the dawn break crooked. But how much more pleasant was the sensation of being a missile without provenance or target, caught up in a tumult of non-Newtonian motion. (112-113)

Yet oddly enough the goal of both men is the same: harmony. Descartes descends reluctantly into the dark, is rescued by the spark of divine grace, and is reborn with a sense of the transcendent unity of knowledge. On the other hand Murphy, dissatisfied with referential forms, willingly moves through the half-light of forms without parallel (the zone in which thought is no longer at the mercy of extension) and into the dark, where both thought and extension dissolve.

Up to the final stage of his journey Murphy has thought of his mind as a closed, bodytight system: yet paradoxically it is his body rather than his mind that transports him beyond the impasse and into the home stretch of the heroic cycle. Murphy would like to be a Geulincxian man and keep his mind insulated from his body, but he cannot. In the zones of light and half-light he is moderately successful, particularly after he leaves Celia—but in the dark, where he is a mote in will-lessness, consciousness and the self no longer exist. Here the Cartesian *cogito* breaks down and chaos itself takes the place of the rational contemplation of chaos. In his own dark Murphy may be free to see himself as a missile without a target, but as soon as he actually moves into the dark and *becomes* that missile, dissolution of the self is inevitable. Murphy has confused knowledge of the quest with the quest itself; in the real dark there is no such thing as Murphy's mind.

Nevertheless, an ironic sort of divine spark illuminates the last movement of Murphy's quest. Like Descartes' bed-chamber, Murphy's garret is filled with sparks of fire. And with the ultimate separation of mind and body Murphy finally experiences an ironic counterpart of Descartes' vision of eternal harmony, as his ashes are dispersed throughout the big world, thereby uniting macro- and microcosm. As a parody of Descartes, Murphy completes the quest.

The other characters of the book are less successful. Celia, who represents the nearest parallel to Murphy, never de-scends below the region of half-light. It is apparently the rocking-chair rather than Murphy's guidance that introduces her to the quest. "She began to understand as soon as he gave up trying to explain." (67) While Murphy is out on the jobpath, Celia spends most of her time "sitting in the rocking-chair with her face to the light. There was not much light, the room devoured it, but she kept her face turned to what there was." (66) Like Murphy, she cannot sit for long in the chair without the impulse stirring to be naked and bound, and although Celia to Murphy remains primarily body, Celia to Celia becomes more and more mind. "She tried to think of

Mr. Kelly or the irrevocable days or the unattainable days, but always the moment came when no effort of thought could prevail against the sensation of being imbedded in a jelly of light." (67) By the time the old boy upstairs dies, Celia has made definite regress in the direction of the half-light. "The footsteps overhead had become part and parcel of her afternoon, with the rocking-chair and the vermigrade wane of light." (134) But after Murphy's death she seems to slide back into the zone of light and extension, and by the end of the book she has returned to the treadmill, where she can only briefly close her eyes to shut out the flood of light.

In contrast to Murphy and Celia, Neary is an indigenous creature of the light, trapped in the zone of Cartesian self-affirmation. Intellectually he is aware of the dark and its influence; when the light in the corridor goes out with a crash, he observes: "There He blows, or I am greatly mistaken." (223) But even though he has knowledge of Murphy's dialectic, he is unwilling to put it to a test. As the narrator remarks,

there seems really little hope for Neary, he seems doomed to hope unending. He has something of Hugo, the fire will not depart from his eye, nor the water from his mouth, as he scratches himself out of one itch into the next, until he shed his mortal mange, supposing that to be permitted. (201-202)

Yet once even Neary seems to drift inadvertently toward the dark zone; a curious feeling comes over him that he will not get through the night alive. Throughout a sleepless night he sits in his chair (such experiences always take place in chairs), gripped by what Jung calls the "perils of the soul," and when Wylie stops in the following afternoon, "Neary's hair was white as snow, but he felt better in himself." (224) Once again the dark has receded, leaving Neary marooned on his island of light.

Wylie and Miss Counihan experience the polarity of light and dark on a more corporeal level. Having neither desire for nor experience of the bodytight mind, they tend to measure all opposites on the pleasure-pain scale. Miss Counihan may parrot Murphy's *mots* for the benefit of her companions (" 'Floodlit the midnight sun?' " [215]), but essentially she sees the dark as a place where people can "meet" and the light as something she can shed on Murphy in order to humiliate Celia. Only once is she confronted with a *chiaroscuro* not of her own making, as she leans out her window to watch Cooper depart. "Bounding the grey pavement, stretching away on either hand beneath the grey span of steps, the areas made a fosse of darkness. The spikes of the railings were a fine saw edge, spurting light." (131) At this sudden exposure to the light and dark she almost falls out the window, but then "Wylie's hands, making two skilful handfuls of her breasts, drew her back to a more social vertigo." (131) From this point onward her vertigo will remain exclusively social.

Wylie prudently avoids all contact with the dark (excepting Miss Counihan's); unlike Murphy he can only see when there is light, and his ostensible goal is a new life for everyone in the light, "the end of darkness for all concerned." (130)

Ticklepenny, Miss Carridge, and Cooper are also heliotropic. Ticklepenny, the ironic bringer of fire to Murphy, also brings light to dispel his darkness; Miss Carridge's guiding light is A.E.'s *The Candle of Vision;* and Cooper's New Jerusalem is the glorious gin-palace which has no need of sun or moon to shine on it. Each time Cooper sees Murphy he must retreat to his fount, and finally, as he is on his way to dump the remains of Murphy,

a burst of music made him halt and turn. It was the pub across the way, opening for the evening session. The lights sprang up in the saloon. . . . The floor was palest ochre, the pin-tables shone like silver . . . the whiskey was in glass tanks, a slow cascando of pellucid yellows. (274)

Mr. Endon's relation to the light and dark is somewhat more complex. As a closed system his is the intellectual dark that Murphy seeks. Yet his ring blazes light in all directions, and on examining his eyes closely Murphy finds their pupils prodigiously dilated, "as though by permanent excess of light." (249) Has Mr. Endon already completed his quest, and passed through the region of the dark to emerge on the other side, reborn as a "wise fool?"[5] Apparently he has—at least Murphy thinks so. But while Murphy malingers in the positive peace of Nothingness following the chess game, Mr. Endon suddenly rises and drifts through the corridors of Skinner's House, "pressing here a light-switch and there an indicator, in a way that seemed haphazard but was in fact determined by an amental pattern as precise as any of those that governed his chess." (246-247) It may seem incongruous that Mr. Endon, the paragon of the closed system, should make use of the big world's instruments of torture to shatter the closed systems of his fellow patients, especially since he has the reputation of being "the most biddable little gaga" in the Mercyseat. In humanistic terms Mr. Endon may be seen as one of the gods who kill us for their sport, but his logic cannot be evaluated by sublunary ethics. We may be sure of only one thing: Mr. Endon's light lies beyond Murphy's darkness.

The polarity of light and dark in *Murphy* operates primarily as a thematic metaphor. Seen in relation to the characters of the book it furnishes a yardstick by which their ideational development may be measured; seen from the standpoint of thematic progression it provides an analogical structure which simultaneously reinforces the narrator and interlocks plot with theme. Serving a somewhat different purpose is the motif of astrology.

Astrology

As the term *motif* implies, astrology is employed for the most part as an aesthetic device. Where the symbolism of light and dark helps to reveal the aesthetic movement of the book as it relates to a given thematic problem, astrology covers the same ground while moving in the opposite direction: it projects the basic thematic issues onto the moving screen of aesthetic development.

It is obvious that a symbol, seen in rhythmic recurrence, can serve as an aesthetic motif, and by the same token a motif, regarded spatially, can become a symbol. The difference between the two is solely one of viewpoint—whether a rectangle is a circle or a circle rectangular depends entirely on where we stand when we look at a cylinder. But if we man the Occamite barricades and insist that a cylinder is nothing but a cylinder, what then is the difference between a symbol and a motif?

Essentially it is a difference of emphasis. Throughout *Murphy* we are reminded that the light and dark are zones of the hero's mind and that his mind is the book's thematic core. Yet at the same time astrology seems to form a metaphorical subcurrent underlying Murphy's quest; and even though it occasionally merges with the light and dark to create a unity of manner and theme, it remains chiefly a stream of analogy running beneath the dramatic surface of the action.

For one thing, it marks off time elapsed. Beckett's narrator is obsessed with the increments of time; not only does he date every major event in the book, he also makes careful notations to indicate the corresponding passage of time in the cosmos. The book opens with "the poor old sun in the Virgin for the billionth time"; (1-2) the evening Celia met Murphy the sun was in Cancer; the following Sunday, when he proposed to her, the moon was in conjunction; when she persuades him to set out on the jobpath the moon is at perigee; when Wylie rescues Neary from the C. G. the sun "passed over into the Balance"; (114) Murphy encounters Austin Ticklepenny on 11 October, "the moon being full again"; (114) Wylie and Miss Counihan decide to set out for London on 7 October, the first day of time's restitution to "the bewitching Miss Greenwich"; (114)[6] and finally, Cooper commits the remains of Murphy to the macrocosm on the evening of 23 October, as the sun moves into Scorpio, zodiacal ruler of the House of Death.

To a limited degree these allusions broaden the book's universe of discourse to include the universe itself. But more importantly, they weave the disparate episodes of the plot into an aesthetically homologous pattern. Seen as theme, astrology is only one of the many panaceas Murphy has sampled; evidently he took it up soon after leaving Neary, because when Celia first met him he was consulting the heavens and a star-chart for June. For a short time the lesser heaven, Celia, prevailed, but only for a short time. By mid-September, when the action of the book begins, Murphy is once again in

need of astral guidance. Yet only a month later, after he has
the opportunity to observe the authentic closed system of Mr.
Endon, he commits astrology to his dustbin of false promises—
by now he is "out of conceit with a system that seemed the
superfluous cartoon of his own." (189) Thematically then
astrology turns out to be only another *cul-de-sac* along Murphy's labyrinthine pilgrimage into darkness. But as an aesthetic device it links the events of his progression in a coherent
sequence.

As Chapter VI adumbrates the thematic significance of
light and dark, so the sixpenny Nativity compiled by Ramas-
wami Krishnaswami Narayanaswami Suk of Berwick Street
paraphrases in pseudo-astrological argot the dramatic events
of the book. This Nativity, commissioned to demonstrate to
Murphy the desirability of marrying Celia and taking a job,
provides an abstract of his movement from West Brompton to
oblivion.

For example: Murphy was born under the sign of Capricorn. This sign is normally associated with the Tenth House,
which rules over the occupation of the native. Suk's main
purpose is after all to put Murphy on the jobpath. The
natural ruler of Capricorn is Saturn, whose nature is described
as "malefic, . . . cold, dry, hard, restricting and masculine.
It rules old age, sorrow, melancholy, disease and chronic ail-
ments, misfortunes, falls, and dark things and places."[7] Although a few of these characteristics seem to fit Murphy quite
well, an important *caveat* must be observed: Murphy says
explicitly that Mercury is his planet, and it may be true, for
Mercury is the planet *par excellence* which transcends the
entire system and has primary influence over the powers of
the mind. As the contradictions in Suk's Nativity suggest,
Murphy may best be seen as Murphy sees himself, as a *causa
sui* encompassing and transcending all the signs and planets.
This may be why the Nativity turns into such a farrago of
zodiacal types: Murphy is warned against Bright's Disease
(Libra) and Grave's Disease (Taurus), his lucky color is
lemon yellow (Taurus) and his lucky gems the amethyst
and diamond (Aries).

"The Moon twenty-three degrees of the Serpent promotes
great Magical Ability of the Eye, to which the lunatic would

easily succumb" (32) proves to be a forecast of Murphy's fateful sight of himself unseen in Mr. Endon's herpetic gaze. "When sensuality rules there is danger of Fits." (33) In a nutshell, Murphy's problem with his body, illustrated by his paroxysmal response to the triple pun. "Great care should be exercised in dealing with publishers, quadrupeds and tropical swamps, as these may terminate unprofitably for the Native." (33) Possibly a sidelong glance at Murphy's encounters with Ticklepenny, Nelly, and Rosie Dew. "Mercury sesquiquadrate with the Anarete is most malefic and will greatly conduce to Success terminating in the height of Glory, which may injure Native's prospects." (33) A perfect description of Murphy's end. Incidentally, it seems quite likely that Mr. Endon should be associated with the Anarete or Eighth House. This is the House of Death; it is ruled by Scorpio, whose type is

fixed, purposeful, magnetic, dominant, jurisdictional. . . . They [Scorpios] are very positive in all their beliefs and willing to die for a purpose. . . . Their plans are farseeing and high-minded. . . . Their deep-seated emotional life sometimes creates a conflict with those near them.[8]

In addition, the colors worn by Mr. Endon are those of Scorpio, dark red and deep crimson.

"The square of Moon and Solar Orb afflicts the Hyleg." (33) Webster's *New International Dictionary* defines hyleg as "the position, occupied by certain planets or parts of signs, from a consideration of which, in its relation to other plane-tary influences, prognostications regarding the life or death of the querent may be made." An hour before Murphy's death, "the moon had been obliged to set, and the sun could not rise for an hour to come." (250-251) "Neptune and Venus in the Bull denotes dealings with the Females only medium de-veloped or of low organic quality." (33) Probably a refer-ence to Murphy's association with Rosie Dew (one of the characteristic occupations for the Neptune type is that of spiritual medium) and Miss Counihan. "Companions or matri-monial Mate are recommended to be born under a fiery triplicity [Aries, Leo, or Sagittarius], when the Bowman should permit of a small family." (33) Obviously Celia is

meant here, because her sixpence bought the services of Suk.
The house ruled by the Bowman governs dreams, visions, and
prophesy; its natives are good-tempered, frank, honest, and
impetuous. Yet in the dramatic structure of the book Celia also
seems readily identifiable with the moon or Venus. Possibly
she, like Murphy, encompasses a wide sector of the zodiac.
At most, the likeness is only suggestive, not definitive. "With
regards to a Career, the Native should inspire and lead, as go
between, promoter, detective, custodian, pioneer or, if possible, explorer." (33) An apt description of Murphy's vocation as quester of the dark.

In this lefthanded manner Murphy's future is forecast.
He notes with approval that "he suffered much with his feet,
and his neck was not altogether free of pain," (75) and when
he meets Ticklepenny and the prognostications of lunatic in
paragraph 2 and custodian in paragraph 7 miraculously
coalesce, the Nativity becomes for him "the poem that he
alone of the living could write." (93) But after coming into
contact with the innumerable closed systems at the M.M.M.,
his sixpence worth of sky changes again, to "the poem that he
alone of all the born could have written." (183) At this
point Murphy has become a preterist, insofar as astrology is
concerned.

A metaphorical association of the various minor characters
with planets and zodiacal signs is suggested by Murphy's
Nativity, but it seems to be only casual, and not a keystone
in the book's aesthetic design. The characters are certainly
types, but their typing follows criteria other than those dictated by the horoscope; that is to say, *Murphy* is essentially
a satire, not a *tour de force* of symbolism. Astrology may be
the most important motif in the book, but it is not permitted
to obliterate theme in consummating its perfection.

Nevertheless, certain questions seem to be answerable only
in terms of astrology. Why, for example, is Miss Carridge
damned by the quality "which the Romans called *caper*,"
(134) if she is not to be identified with Capricorn? As Wylie
says, " 'she is at hand, . . . unless there is a real goat in the
house as well.' " (235) And why should there be twin Clinches
if they are not the Gemini?

But even if such relationships as these are valid, they may be acknowledged only as incidental organizing devices, not as retractors by means of which the book is to be pried open and anatomized. Individually the characters may be neatly classified and distributed throughout the zodiac, but seen tangentially in relation to one another (as they must be, if such identifications are to be given any thematic importance), they form no significant pattern. Too many qualifications enter in: once characters have been dissected according to element, sex, part of body, color, gem, physiognomy, occupation, triplicity, cross, house, rulership, exaltation, detriment, fall, and so on, they become stylized out of existence.

Yet in terms of aesthetic movement the book does trace out a clear zodiacal pattern. As the following diagram indicates, the stations of Murphy's journey through the plot may be seen to occupy, in sequence, each of the twelve houses of the zodiac, beginning with the House of the Native, here the cusp of Aries at 270°, and proceeding counterclockwise through the circle.

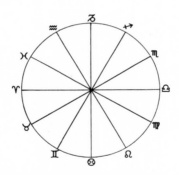

1. The Native: introduction to Murphy.
2. Money, movable possessions: the rocking-chair, Suk's Nativity (which sends Murphy in search of money).
3. Short journeys: daily rounds on the jobpath.
4. Home: Murphy and Celia establish residence in Brewery Road.
5. Pleasure: serenade, nocturne, and aubade with Celia.
6. Food and clothing, illness: Murphy's non-porous suit, loss of cookies to Nelly, Rosie Dew's panpygoptosis.

7. Contracts: Murphy agrees to assume Ticklepenny's duties at the M.M.M.
8. Death: suicide of the old boy upstairs.
9. Long journeys: Murphy leaves Celia for the M.M.M.
10. Occupation: Murphy begins work at the M.M.M.
11. Friends: Mr. Endon.
12. Sorrow: Murphy dies; Celia mourns.

The Chess Game

Throughout *Murphy* astrology and light/darkness, systole and diastole of the book's symbolic structure, operate to display theme in motion and to arrange aesthetic movement in a coherent spatial pattern. Serving a more limited function is the chess game between Murphy and Mr. Endon. Its symbolic values are much easier defined than those of the broader analogical systems, chiefly because its jurisdiction is wholly spatial: its significance is revealed within the eighty-six moves of the game.

The chess game may be seen thematically as the interaction of a perfect closed system with an imperfect one, or aesthetically as a gauge of the distance separating Murphy from his ideal, Mr. Endon. While Murphy attacks, reconsiders, withdraws, and attacks again, continually at cross purposes with himself, Mr. Endon plays with a remarkable fixity of intent; his game, dictated by the amental logic of the closed system, is a brilliant *coup de repos*.

"Endon's Affence" is a perfect illustration of the microcosm in action. While advancing no more than two pawns (the only pieces which can never return to the ideal deployment of the game not yet underway), Mr. Endon succeeds in turning his king row inside out—with the exception of the troublesome rooks—and bringing it back into proper order, thereby closing the circle. Moreover, throughout this virtuoso performance he at no time captures a piece or allows himself to be put in check, and only once gives any indication whatever that he is aware of his opponent's existence.

It would seem that such a game might be easily emulated, and Murphy tries to do just this. But by means of his inspired *début*, the "Pipe-opener," Mr. Endon gets a jump on Murphy and then covers his tracks with diabolic skill.

Murphy, who plays White, makes his first error with his first move; P-K4 will prevent him from patterning his game on that of his opponent. Mr. Endon's counter however (Kt-KR3) is a fine illustration of the subtitle of his game, *Zweispringerspott*, for only by employing his knights to make breathing room in his king row will he be able to execute the intricate manoeuvre he has planned. Within four moves Mr. Endon has used Murphy's ill-fated pawn to capture the lead. Murphy, unable to follow his master, must now venture out on his own—and here his troubles begin to increase.

After testing Murphy's strength with the Pipe-opener, Mr. Endon recalls his knights and starts the game in earnest. Incidentally, with his eighth move Mr. Endon has once again achieved absolute symmetry of deployment; by the end of the game he will have performed this feat no less than six times. The flux of forms in his closed system always comes to rest in perfect harmony. Murphy makes his next serious blunder with his tenth move (P-KKt3), which will hinder his progress throughout the rest of the game. Mr. Endon realizes better the necessity of keeping a way cleared for the knights; his eleventh and twelfth moves (Kt-KKt3 and B-K2) once again put obstacles in the way of Murphy's knight-play and cause him to fall even further behind. Mr. Endon's thirteenth move (P-Q3) marks his final commitment of the game—he now has sufficient working space. At this stage Murphy is still trying in vain to make up for lost moves. By his sixteenth play, Mr. Endon already has reversed the positions of his king and queen, a *coup* Murphy is never to achieve. Two moves later Murphy has almost despaired of following his opponent's game; and as the deployment of his pieces becomes more and more chaotic, Mr. Endon withdraws once again into the flawless symmetry of his closed system. Still trying to catch up, Murphy finds he must commit yet another pawn in order to clear a path for his queen's bishop (move twenty-one) and by the twenty-sixth move he must make a further advance in order to bring back his knight (P-QKt4).

Finally Murphy abandons hope of emulating the Endon Affence and tries frantically to invade the closed system. But

Mr. Endon's microcosm is blandly impermeable. At the twenty-seventh move Murphy's scattered troops once more face the inscrutable symmetry of Mr. Endon's king row— QKt, QR, K, QB, KB, Q, KR and KKt. Murphy tries to forestall the *Zweispringer* stratagem, without success. By now he is his own worst enemy.

Then, as Mr. Endon signals his victory by symbolically queening his rooks, Murphy abandons his fitful offensive and launches a suicide attack with his king. This disturbs the Affence not in the least; Mr. Endon begins his inexorable retirement. Incidentally, here the only flaw in his microcosmic game takes place—he is compelled to put Murphy momentarily in check (move thirty-six). Wavering in his attack, Murphy attempts to clear the return trip of his queen; then, at his thirty-sixth move he resumes the abject offensive with his king and king's knight. In a last-ditch stand Murphy tries to keep his opponent from making the fatal exchange of king and queen (move forty-one). When this manoeuvre fails he can only mark time with his king and watch on helplessly while Mr. Endon executes his concluding solitaire.

Yellow

Light and darkness objectify theme; astrology serves as an organizing metaphor; the chess game furnishes a visible analogy for a specific thematic problem—now to balance the ledger with a limited aesthetic motif: the color yellow.

If the chess game is ancillary to the broad metaphorical system of light/darkness, its purpose being to figure forth a specific view of the microcosm, then yellow may be similarly regarded as an element of the general aesthetic motif of astrology. Whereas astrological references chart out the overall course of the book, yellow provides us with a series of fixes along the way. Also, as the chess game displays its symbolic purpose in spatial terms, so the yellow functions chiefly in time and motion. It reveals itself only through patterned repetition, and no unique semeiotic value may be assigned to it. Each of the symbols and motifs seen up to here has had its analogical sphere of influence rather clearly defined— light/darkness (108-113), astrology (32-33), chess (243-245)

—but yellow stands as one side of an open equation, to be completed by the reader.

Seen in relation to the character of Murphy, yellow might appear to be nothing more than another element in the astrological framework. Since yellow is his lucky color, according to Suk, it is not surprising that he should choose a flat with walls of vivid lemon or wear a bow tie of the same shade. But yellow seems to have a wider range of meaning for Murphy. For one thing, it is the color of his complexion, perpetually liable to waning in moments of stress. On seeing his Nativity, "All the colour (yellow) had ebbed from his face"; (31) when Celia suggests that he go out to look for a job, "Murphy lost all his yellow again"; (38) and finally, when it seems that he must give up his garret in the M.M.M. for want of heat, "he broke into a sweat, lost all his yellow." (164)

In general thematic terms, yellow seems to represent a flaw or decay of some sort: "In the days when Murphy was concerned with seeing Miss Counihan, he had had to close his eyes to do so. And even now when he closed them there was no guarantee that Miss Counihan would not appear. That was Murphy's really yellow spot." (90)[9] Incidentally, Miss Counihan is also Neary's yellow spot. Driven to despair by her vacillating affections ("she could no more welcome his arrival at her hotel than green, yellow, green is a legitimate sequence of traffic lights" [55]), he comes to the conclusion that if Cooper fails him he will post himself outside her hotel and as she comes by, "take salts of lemon." (55)

Celia too is susceptible to yellow. After the old boy upstairs has died, she goes into a state of shock: "the clear green of her eyes . . . was silted with yellow." (137) Even for Ticklepenny yellow is a reminder of his weakness; now that he is on the water wagon, he must make do with lemon-phosphate.

Cooper alone seems able to reconcile himself with his weakness. The only thing that prevents him from indulging it is the price of a drink, and when Neary furnishes this, he immediately comes to terms with his yellow, in the public house where "the floor was palest ochre, . . . the whiskey was in glass tanks, a slow cascando of pellucid yellows." (274)

The Magdalen Mental Mercyseat

One more element of symbolic structure may be mentioned here: the Magdalen Mental Mercyseat. Strictly speaking, the M.M.M. is neither symbol nor motif, although it partakes of both—it is rather a complex or focal point where the major themes converge to provide a backdrop for Murphy's final appearance. Almost every prognostication in Suk's Nativity seems to point towards the M.M.M.: here the light and dark are seen in starkest contrast, here the fateful chess game is played, and here Murphy finally abandons astrology.

As well as uniting the various symbolic constituents of the book, the M.M.M. also marks the last stage of Murphy's journey. Seen in terms of his movement through the zodiac, it may be equated with the house of Pisces, combining the asylum with the cloister. The Twelfth House is the house of bondage, both enforced and voluntary; therefore, the native may be seen here either as a prisoner or a monk. As its name implies, the Magdalen Mental Mercyseat is an ironic inversion of a monastery. At its head is the nepotist Bim Clinch, the most "resolute and successful pope to his family in the south of England." (166) Located between two counties, it is for Murphy also a way-station between two worlds.

Murphy comes here to seek the transcendent peace of the closed system, along with 85 per cent of the inmates, for only a select 15 per cent have been certified as the chosen people—the rest are lay brothers. The activities of the patients are unmistakably monkish: "melancholics, motionless and brooding, holding their heads or bellies according to type. Paranoids, feverishly covering sheets of paper with complaints against their treatment or verbatim reports of their inner voices." (167-168) Even the practices of the staff members bring to mind the more notorious mediaeval monasteries: "No female nurse had taken a male nurse to husband within living memory, though one had once been almost obliged to." (161)

The *sanctum sanctorum* of the M.M.M. is Skinner's House, where "the battle raged most fiercely . . . between the psychotic and psychiatric points of view." (165) Quite instinctively Murphy homes on Skinner's House like a carrier pigeon. Its wards consist of two corridors, "intersecting to form a T, or more correctly a decapitated potence, the three extremities developed into spacious crutch-heads, which were the read-ing-, writing- and recreation-rooms or 'wrecks.' " (166) Here we find a triple-barreled ambiguity. The term *potence* may apply to (1) the crutch-cross, (2) a gallows, or (3) the *Potenz* as used by Schelling to designate the gradation from physical to spiritual existence. It is interesting to note that the eastern end of the potence is incomplete; since Gothic cathe-drals were normally built facing eastward, this means that the nave or cross has been decapitated.

In spite of its shortcomings, as far as Murphy is concerned the M.M.M. is an empyrean; it is his "dungeon in Spain." (180) He sees in the impassive schizoids hope for the future, and in the padded cell a potential bower of bliss:

The three dimensions, slightly concave, were so exquisitely proportioned that the absence of a fourth was scarcely felt. The tender luminous oyster-grey of the pneumatic upholstery, cushioning every square inch of ceiling, walls, floor and door, lent colour to the truth, that one was a prisoner of air. The temperature was such that only total nudity could do it justice. (181)

For Murphy the pads fulfill the promise only hinted at by his rocking-chair. In a pad he would no longer need to con-strain his body by means of scarves, the unvarying climate would enable him to do away with his non-porous suit for-ever, and there would be no more danger of unanticipated crucifixions, such as the one described in Chapter III. Never-theless, he soon learns that the pad has its flaws, such as the judas window where the sane eye appears at regular intervals day and night, and the light-switch used by staff members periodically to flood the closed system with a thousand-watt glare. But most objectionable of all is the therapeutic method of the psychiatrists:

The function of treatment was to bridge the gulf, translate the sufferer from his own pernicious dungheap to the glorious world of discrete particles, where it would be his inestimable preroga-tive once again to wonder, love, hate, desire, rejoice and howl in a reasonably balanced manner, and comfort himself with the society of others in the same predicament. (177)

Murphy's blindest spot is his supposition that all the patients are having a wonderful time, although finally he is forced to concede that at least one maniac is the "epitome of all the self-made plutolaters who ever triumphed over empty pockets and clean hands." (168) Nonetheless, he still clings to the belief that the melancholic's depression and the paranoid's despair are due solely to the intervention of the doctors. In the last analysis, it is only Mr. Endon who fulfils all Murphy's requirements of the microcosm; but as we have seen, Mr. Endon's system is so impervious to the world outside that even Murphy cannot penetrate it.

The M.M.M. is quite literally Murphy's last resort. The negative vision of the microcosm, epitomized by the Geulincxian tag *Ubi nihil vales, ibi nihil velis* has offered no lasting satisfaction, and the rocking-chair has failed to dispel his deplorable susceptibility to Celia and ginger cookies. So he plunges into the M.M.M. with a hope born of despair: "Suppose he were to clinch it now, in the service of the Clinch clan! That would indeed be very pretty." (179) His first day of duty gives him cause for blatant optimism. Success with the patients leads him to attribute Suk's prophesy, "great Magical Ability of the Eye to which the lunatic would easily succumb," (32) to his own powers, and to see in it a harbinger of future bliss. (He has not yet encountered the Endon eye.) "It meant that they felt in him what they had been and he in them what he would be. It meant that nothing less than a slap-up psychosis could consummate his life's strike." (184) Even his garret seems a perfect spot to complete the quest, once heating arrangements have been made.[10]

Night duty, however, soon dampens Murphy's optimism. During the day he had been content to observe and mingle with the patients, to imagine himself one of them, but at night he finds himself shut out and left to his own devices. "In short there was nothing but he, the unintelligible gulf and they. That was all. All. ALL." (240) And after seeing this gulf mirrored in Mr. Endon's eyes, he tries desperately to retreat to the light. But now even Celia, his most persistent "yellow spot," will not appear to him, and darkness falls.

Chapter IV

Style

HERE an apparent contradiction in terms arises. Since style is usually regarded as *how* a writer expresses himself, and consequently is treated as an element solely of manner, how is it to be parcelled out among the three large groups of matter, manner, and theme? The difficulty here may be traced to the essentially Romantic view of style which has prevailed for the last century and a half. Insofar as the personality of the author is used as a lens through which his work is examined, then it is true that style means nothing more than self-expression; but such a viewpoint restricts the critic's field of vision unnecessarily, in that it forces upon him the burden of proving sincerity and intent. So once again a broader definition seems worth while.

Style seen as matter is the proper hunting-ground of the linguist and the literary detective, since it concerns the relation of the written word to the history of language and literary convention. At this level the biography of the writer demonstrates its usefulness; here for example one may cite Beckett's use of Belacqua in his early poems and short stories.[1] But here also intrudes the gremlin of the biographical specialist —the temptation to base assertions pertaining to theme on this sort of evidence. Ultimately such explication can only lead one away from the work and toward the life of its author. For example: the different manner in which death is treated by Camus and Hemingway can be "explained" in terms of Camus' attack of tuberculosis as a child and Hemingway's brush with violent death in war—but the only thing proved by evidence from such sources is the fact that in all likelihood Hemingway did not write *La Peste* nor Camus *A Farewell to Arms*. Nothing whatever has been said about the aesthetic or thematic uses of death in the two novels.

Style seen as matter is valuable also in the determination of genre; the concordance and the linguistic examination take their places here as documents testifying to the literary and linguistic conventions employed in the work. I have said that *Murphy* seems to fall within the extraverted and intellectualized universe of the Menippean satire: a word study of the book should indicate that it is far more intellectually oriented than most novels, and a rhetorical analysis should point out that preciosity of expression which has always been a trademark of satire. In lieu of such undertakings here, perhaps a glance at some of the allusions in *Murphy* will reflect in brief the literary and intellectual background of the work.

As is common among examples of the genre, *Murphy* is adamantly literary in its outlook. Among the writers named, quoted, or misquoted are: Dante (77, 78), Marlowe (221), Fletcher (49), Boswell (167), Swift (139), Blake (70), Burns (261), Wordsworth (100, 106), Shelley (99), Mary Shelley (124), Hugo (201), George Moore (216), Malraux (156), George Russell (155), and Balzac (228). Also of interest to the Beckett scholar is the casual reference to Watt (81) and the Engels sisters, (228, 229) Moran's neighbors in *Molloy*. Of the allusions listed above, only two are given to Murphy, one to Rosie Dew, two to Miss Counihan, and one to the coroner—the rest are all made by the narrator. Most of them are ironic and incidental—Miss Counihan's adaptation of Marlowe to her own purpose is typical: "'Who ever met . . . that met not at first sight?'" (221) Only Malraux and Dante are used with broad thematic intent.

Among the non-literary artists cited in *Murphy*, a preponderance are Renaissance painters and sculptors: Tintoretto (140), Parmigianino (101), Barlach (239), Puget (239), and Bellini. (251) The only contemporary artist mentioned is Braque. (63) In his perception Murphy is an ironic Renaissance man; he visualizes the triple pun in terms of Tintoretto's *Origin of the Milky Way*, and his final vision in the rocking-chair, when the figures of immediate experience fail him, is that of "the clenched fists and rigid upturned face of the Child in a Giovanni Bellini circumcision, waiting to feel the knife."

Serving as an ironic underpinning to the intellectual bias of the book, eleven philosophers are either mentioned or indirectly alluded to in *Murphy*: Pythagoras (5, 47, 50, 59, 90), Democritus (246), Socrates (200), Spinoza (107), Geulincx (178), Leibnitz (181), Descartes (140), Berkeley (58), Newton (113, 201), Hegel (222), and Sartre (168). Here Neary takes the lead; of the eleven allusions, five are either made by or about him. The rest are made by the narrator, chiefly with regard to the philosophical implications of Murphy's quest. References to philosophy appear quite often in ironic and occasional contexts, yet they seem in general to be more central thematically than those of literary provenience. The tags from Geulincx and Spinoza serve well to summarize Murphy's dilemma; the distinction between Neary the Newtonian and Murphy caught up in a "tumult of non-Newtonian motion" (113) is apt; and the description of the padded cell in Leibnitzian terms (181) throws an ironic shadow directly across Murphy's questpath. Yet Descartes, one of the principal thematic sources of the book, is mentioned only via the "dream of Descartes linoleum" in the flat on Brewery Road. Incidentally, it is interesting to observe that of the eleven philosophers named above, more than half are representatives of the Age of Reason. A more appropriate backdrop for Murphy's quest could not be desired.

Among the medical authorities mentioned in *Murphy*, all, with the exception of Alkmaion, are either psychologists or neurologists: Koffka (48), Külpe (80), Bühler (81), Marbe (81), Korsakoff (168), and Freud (218). Since the book may be seen thematically as a case-history of Murphy's mind, their appearance is not altogether unexpected. Moreover, in the inner quest, psychology (and especially its stepchild, psychoanalysis) represents the modern continuation of Pascalian introspection and links art and philosophy with religion. To a great extent the couch has replaced the confessional and the porch.

Besides Christ, six Biblical characters are mentioned, but only in a casual manner: Job and his "fragments" Bildad and Zophar (70), Lazarus (180), Luke (215) and Matthew (215).

In the introduction to this essay it was noted that style as manner concerns itself with literal, as opposed to descriptive, meaning. Applied to any given work of literature, the study of style as an aesthetic implement demands that the critic temporarily endeavor to prune away the undergrowth of conventional sign-values attached to words, leaving only a minimum of external meaning with which to begin his work. Now it is obvious that this denudation of meaning can only be partial—otherwise the language of the work would be incomprehensible. How much residual meaning to leave intact is up to the discretion of the critic, guided only by the demands of the work. Some works of fiction are content to rely almost wholly on descriptive language; others insist on establishing their own patterns of meaning. For example, *An American Tragedy* rests firmly on the bedrock of descriptive meaning, but *Tender Buttons* can be read only with reference to *Tender Buttons*.

Throughout *Murphy* the narrator signals the appearance of literal language. The use of "yellow" has already been observed. The fact that yellow is a motif and creates its significance through varied repetition illustrates the manner in which literal meaning is established. Literal language normally defines itself through recurrence in context, and a recognizable pattern must appear before any part of it yields up its meaning.

Frequently such patterns are employed to provide mock euphemisms, as Beckett does a saltarello around the censors. The verb "meet," for example:

[Celia:]   I won't come back. . . . I won't open your letters.
             I'll move my pitch. . . . I'll be sorry I met you.
[Murphy:]   *Met* me! . . . Met is magnificent. (35-36)

"But have I not said," said Neary, "now we can part? Surely that is a great advantage."

"Do you really mean to sit there and tell me," said Miss Counihan, "*me*, that you consider we are now met?"

Wylie covered his ears, threw back his head and cried:

"Stop it! Or is it too late?"

High above his head he tossed his arms, set off in a rapid shuffle, seized Miss Counihan's hands, raised them gently clear of her rump. In a moment they would hit the trail.

"Who ever met," said Miss Counihan, not in the least perturbed apparently, "if it comes to that, that met not at first sight?"

"There is only one meeting and parting," said Wylie. "The act of love."

"Fancy that!" said Miss Counihan. (221)

Similar structures of literal meaning may be observed in the words "passions," "music," and "all out." One of the most interesting is Murphy's digression on the etymology of "gas." During his first night in the garret he explodes the discrete meanings which have become associated with "gas" and "chaos" and considers them in their original state of identity:

And the etymology of gas? Could it be the same word as chaos? Hardly. Chaos was yawn. But then cretin was Christian. Chaos would do, it might not be right but it was pleasant, for him henceforward gas would be chaos, and chaos gas. (175)

He has bridged the gulf to oblivion; next he reflects on the inadequacy of gas/chaos:

It could make you yawn, warm, laugh, cry, cease to suffer, live a little longer, die a little sooner. What could it not do? Gas. Could it turn a neurotic into a psychotic? No. Only God could do that. Let there be a Heaven in the midst of the waters, let it divide the waters from the waters. The Chaos and Waters Facilities Act. The Chaos, Light and Coke Co. Hell. Heaven. Helen. Celia. (175-176)

By now gas has assumed connotations of both life and death; but as Murphy realizes, it cannot resolve his quest. Divine grace must separate the waters of chaos to transform him into a microcosm (he does not know that his quest is soon to be fulfilled with the aid of gas). Symbolically he creates order out of chaos, by postulating the appearance of hell and heaven. Then, in an almost Joycean portmanteau, the two are collapsed into "Helen," with all her literary associations, who in turn becomes Murphy's hell-heaven, Celia. As usual, his thoughts sweep out into the dark, only to return to Celia and the demands of his body.

In this way the annunciation is made to Murphy. After the dream he has a vague "postmonition of calamity" and the groundwork is laid for his final excursion into chaos. In his last rocking-chair session Murphy can no longer summon up the image of Celia to dispel chaos, with the result that "the gas went on in the w.c., excellent gas, superfine chaos. Soon his body was quiet." (253)

By such means, patterns of literal meaning are formed. More important however to the theme of *Murphy* is the negative side of this process, the breakdown of descriptive language. For example, the word-thing relationship is frequently called into question: the normally stable equation of noun and referent gradually disintegrates as the book progresses. Neary's golden mean of heart control, for instance: "It was the mediation between these extremes that Neary called the Apmonia. When he got tired of calling it the Apmonia he called it the Isonomy. When he got sick of the sound of Isonomy he called it the Attunement." (3-4) And as he names it, it ceases to exist.

Murphy too questions the word-thing relationship: "What passed for a garret in Great Britain and Ireland was really nothing more than an attic. An attic! How was it possible for such a confusion to arise? A basement was better than an attic. An attic!" (162) And the narrator casts doubt on the possibility of accurate descriptive meaning in his portrayal of Skinner's House: "There were no open wards in the ordinary sense, but single rooms, or as some would say, cells, or as Boswell said, mansions, opening south off the nave and east and west off the transepts." (167) In this way a gap is created between language and being, between the names of things and things themselves.

The same procedure is followed with regard to all communication. The narrator begins to take words to task quite early in the book:

He [Murphy] sat in his chair in this way because it gave him pleasure! First it gave his body pleasure, it appeased his body. Then it set him free in his mind. For it was not until his body was appeased that he could come alive in his mind. . . . And life in his mind gave him pleasure, such pleasure that pleasure was not the word. (2)

The movement here is obvious: first a simple positive statement is made, which is subsequently qualified, and finally thrown out altogether. Such a pattern of collapse may be ob-

served throughout the book. For example: "Having gone to
sleep, though sleep was hardly the word . . ." (29) and when
Wylie tries to explain what women see in Murphy:

> "It is his—" stopping for want of the right word. There
> seemed to be for once, a right word.
> "His what?" said Neary. . . .
> "His surgical quality," said Wylie.
> It was not quite the right word. (62)[2]

The "right word" simply does not exist in *Murphy*.
Even in the most commonplace situations all language is found
to be essentially literal, and points only to the chasm between
words and things. Throughout the book are signalled the
weaknesses that words are heir to through ambiguities, puns,
awkward phrasings, unavoidable repetitions—all the purely
mechanical obstacles every user of language has to cope with.
For example: "Some public baths are called mixed where the
bathing is not." (165) And "This was a balloon that Neary
quickly punctured, with a sketch of the phases through which
the young aspirant in London had to pass before he could call
himself an old suspirant." (53)

The stylistic awkwardness inherent in a consistent point of
view is also signalled by the narrator's perpetual movement
in and out of the action. In the midst of the dramatic development, he often throws in a gloss; in the following passage
we see the puncturing of situation coupled with a casual back-
hand to the censors:

> Celia said that if he did not find work at once she would
> have to go back to hers. Murphy knew what that meant. No
> more music.
> This phrase is chosen with care, lest the filthy censors should
> lack an occasion to commit their filthy synecdoche. (76)

Similarly, during Neary's night of peril,

> he simply had this alarming conviction that every second was
> going to announce itself the first of his last ten minutes or a
> quarter of an hour on earth. The number of seconds in one
> dark night is a simple calculation that the curious reader will
> work out for himself. (224)[3]

This leads directly into the thematic use of style in *Murphy*, for the aesthetic and thematic levels overlap here to such an extent that they are practically identical. The situation occurs because the primary argument which style puts forward refers to itself. In other words, it is language testifying to the inadequacy of language.

In his study of style and theme, Niklaus Gessner lists the following devices employed to emphasize inadequacy (*Unzulänglichkeit*):

1. Misunderstanding (*Missverständnis*)
2. Monolog
3. Formulaic speech (*feste Redewendung*)
4. Telegrammatic style (*Telegrammstil*)
5. Search for the right word (*Suche nach dem richtigen Wort*)
6. Congeries (*Worthäufung*)
7. Juxtaposition of synonyms (*Gegenüberstellung von Synonymen*)
8. Overemphasis (*Überbetonung*)
9. Word-chaos (*Wortchaos*)
10. Meaningless punctuation (*ausdruckslose Interpunktion*)

Although he uses these devices primarily to measure the extent of stylistic disintegration in *En attendant Godot*, a number of them may also be found in *Murphy*.

Misunderstandings constitute the rationale of social interaction: Murphy cannot understand Mr. Endon, nor Mr. Kelly, Celia, nor the minor characters Murphy—in fact, the only characters who seem to understand one another are Neary, Wylie, and Miss Counihan. Even Celia, who is nearest Murphy, is at a loss to understand him:

She looked at him helplessly. He seemed serious. But he had seemed serious when he spoke of putting on his gems and lemon, etc. She felt, as she felt so often with Murphy, spattered with words that went dead as soon as they sounded; each word obliterated, before it had time to make sense, by the word that came next; so that in the end she did not know what had been said. It was like difficult music heard for the first time. (40)

As Gessner observes, there are no formal monologues in *Murphy*. For generically determined reasons the narrator

assumes the burden of character revelation, and the inade-
quacies of language are brought out in his commentary more
than by the characters themselves.

In the category of formulaic speech Gessner cites Miss
Counihan's mid-Victorian vocabulary: " 'Oh, if you have,'
cried Miss Counihan, 'if you have news of my love, speak,
speak I adjure you.' " (119) Here he observes that "im
Frühwerk *Murphy* werden . . . die formelhaften Ausdrücke
den sprechenden Personen in den Mund gelegt. Das erzählende
Subjekt verwendet sie selber noch nicht."[4] Yet the same sac-
charine style is frequently used by the narrator when Miss
Counihan enters the action: "She was set aside for Murphy,
who had torn himself away to set up for his princess, in some
less desolate quarter of the globe, a habitation meet for her."
(50-51) And later, when she begs Neary not to open his door
to Wylie, she "threw herself on Neary's mercy, not by word
of mouth, obviously, but with bended knee, panting bosom,
clasped hands, passion-dimmed belladonna, etc." (209)

All this points less to the superficial denigration of style
through cliché than to a basic opposition of language to
reality. It demonstrates once again the illusory layer of order
that language imposes on being.

Instances of telegrammatic style as nursery-talk (*"Klein-
kindersprache"*)[5] are not to be found in *Murphy;* the theme
of incommunicability is pointed out chiefly by the narrator
through exposition rather than by the characters dramatically.
Yet a prototype of the endless telegrammatic conversations of
Estragon and Vladimir in *En attendant Godot* may be seen in
the disjunctive epigrams of Neary, Wylie, and Miss Counihan:

> "Coleridge-Taylor played with feeling?" said Wylie.
> "A perfume thrown on the horehound?" said Miss Counihan.
> "The guillotine sterilized?" said Wylie.
> "Floodlit the midnight sun?" said Miss Counihan.
> "We look on the dark side," said Neary. "It is undeniably
> less trying to the eyes." (215)

Again we see each character as a relatively closed system,
conscious only of his own immediate needs and impervious to
communication from the outside.

The search for the right word has already been pointed out in Wylie's effort to formulate the source of Murphy's charm. Gessner also cites within this category the police-blotter description of Celia in Chapter II, with the observation that

das richtige Wort, das sich beim Leser in eine Anschauung der zu beschreibenden Frau verwandeln würde, bleibt unauffindbar und die Beschreibung kann nur mit Hilfe abstrakter Zahlen erreicht werden, wodurch wieder gezeigt wird, dass die Sprache auch in diesem Bereich des Ausdrucks, nämlich im Bereich der Beschreibung und Schilderung, ein unzulängliches Mittel ist.[6]

This may be true up to a point, but if language is inadequate for the purpose of description, how can numbers be of any help? Most important here is again the gulf separating style and meaning. Celia may be the leading lady of the book, but she is introduced in the most detached manner possible; here style forces ironic distance upon the reader and obliges him to see her stripped of the empathy normally associated with characters in a novel.

There are no congeries of words in *Murphy* to compare with those of the later works, but occasionally the tendency does crop up, as in the description of Cooper's hands (207) or the character of the male nurses at the M.M.M. (238) or the jobpath (138), and particularly in the list of artists to be seen on the Strand:

writers, underwriters, devils, ghosts, columnists, musicians, lyricists, organists, painters and decorators, sculptors and statuaries, critics and reviewers, major and minor, drunk and sober, laughing and crying, in schools and singly, passed up and down. (14-15)

The satirical word-play here is apparent, but more important is the purpose it serves. In comparing the congeries in Beckett with those in Rabelais, Gessner sums up their thematic effects quite well.

Bei Rabelais waren es Wortexplosionen; es war die unbändige Freude an den neuentdeckten Mitteln und Möglichkeiten der Sprache. Bei Beckett geht es darum, das unbrauchbar gewordene Wort lächerlich zu machen. Es ist—wie Beckett selber einmal sagte—"le dénigrement comique du mot."[7]

As with congeries of words, Beckett's juxtaposition of synonyms to point up the insufficiencies of language does not reach in *Murphy* the level of the boldly meaningless it attains in his later works. Nevertheless, occasional examples of this technique do appear, as in Neary's definition of the *aurum mediocritas* of heart control (3-4) and the narrator's description of the rooms/cells/mansions of Skinner's House. (167)

The process of overemphasis is already well advanced in *Murphy*, as witnessed by the structures of literal meaning formed by the verb "meet" and the numerous permutations. Like the other stylistic devices mentioned here, overemphasis, through incessant repetition, demolishes the customary sign values of words.[8]

There are no instances of verborrhea or meaningless punctuation in *Murphy* such as may be found in the later writings, but none should be expected here, for it is only with the breakdown of the ironic distance between narrator and character that such stylistic tricks become practicable. Like the monologue, verborrhea and meaningless punctuation await the interior narration of *Watt* and the trilogy.

A number of entries may be added to Gessner's list of techniques which lend ironic distortion and signal the collapse of communication:

1. Meiosis: Murphy has had a heart attack while sleeping; Celia rushes in to find him overturned in his rocking-chair with blood gushing from his nose. " 'Help,' said Murphy." (29)

2. Pun: Murphy describes Suk's Nativity as his " 'life warrant' " and "bull of incommunication" (31); following its advice he remains "constantly on his guard against the various threats to his Hyleg and whole person generally" (75); his final utterance is described by the narrator as an "afflatulence." (250)

3. Euphemism: " 'Uric acid,' said Neary." (211)

4. Aposiopesis: " 'Have fire in this garret before night or—' " (164)

5. Portmanteau word: " 'A decayed valet severs the connexion and you set up a niobaloo.' " (138-139)

With the breakdown of conversation into a series of disconnected statements, meaning can be transmitted only by means of the most rudimentary system of communication, sign language. By gesture Celia first establishes contact with Murphy and Wylie clarifies his intentions toward Miss Counihan, and through facial expression alone Cooper is able to show

the finest shades of irresolution, revulsion, doglike devotion, cat-like discretion, fatigue, hunger, thirst and reserves of strength, in a very small fraction of the time that the finest oratory would require for a greatly inferior evasion, and without exposing its proprietor to misquotation. (205)

But even gesture is not always effective. Mr. Kelly tries in vain to assume the position of the thinker and Neary fails miserably in an effort to resolve his unfinished gesture. Only Mr. Endon eludes the dilemma, by denying its existence and suspending gesture as much as possible.

One more stylistic device must be mentioned here: the musical development of thematic variations. Neary's letters to Wylie and Miss Counihan have relatively little thematic interest, serving only to reemphasize the static quality of the puppet show, but the Parthian shots of Celia and Murphy are more significant; each of them describes in capsule form the final position taken by the speaker. It is at this point that ironic distance collapses. When Neary, Wylie, and Miss Counihan visit Celia, she sums up her relationship to Murphy in this manner: " 'At first I thought I had lost him because I could not take him as he was. Now I do not flatter myself.' " Here both subject and answer are introduced together. After a rest, the answer is presented alone: " 'I was a piece out of him that he could not go on without, no matter what I did.' " Another rest, followed by restatement of the subject in terms of Murphy's quest: " 'He had to leave me to be what he was before he met me, only worse, or better, no matter what I did.' " Then a long rest, followed by the resolution: " 'I was the last exile.' A rest. 'The last, if we are lucky.' " (234) And as we have seen, she is and they are.

Soon afterwards Murphy delivers his peroration. Here the development is that of the variation rather than the fugue. A theme is introduced briefly:

"the last at last seen of him
himself unseen by him
and of himself"

After a rest it is repeated with pronominal ambiguities cleared
up: " 'The last Mr. Murphy saw of Mr. Endon was Mr. Murphy unseen by Mr. Endon. This was also the last Murphy saw
of Murphy.' " After another rest, it is again restated—this time
with both ambiguity and tautology eliminated—to poor effect:
" 'The relation between Mr. Murphy and Mr. Endon could
not have been better summed up than by the former's sorrow
at seeing himself in the latter's immunity from seeing anything
but himself.' "[9] Through this accretion of descriptive language
meaning has become murkier than ever, but the problem is
ultimately resolved by a well-chosen metaphor: " 'Mr. Murphy
is a speck in Mr. Endon's unseen.' " (250)

Notes

Introduction

1. Princeton, N. J., 1957.
2. Cf. Joseph Campbell, *The Hero With A Thousand Faces*, New York (1949) and Otto Rank, *The Myth of the Birth of the Hero and Other Writings*, New York (1959).
3. *Aspects of the Novel*, New York (1927), p. 161.
4. *Op. cit.*, p. 74.
5. Dante explains the relationship in this manner:
   Cosi parlar conviensi al vostro ingegno;
   Perocchè solo da sensato apprende
   Cio, che fa poscia d'intelletto degno.
   Per questo la Scrittura condiscende
   A vostra facultate, e piedi e mano
   Attribuisce a Dio, ed altro intende.
   —*Paradiso* IV, 11. 40-45.
6. *Op. cit.*, p. 309.

I. Form

1. New York, n.d., p. 253. Page numbers of subsequent citations from *Murphy* will be given in parentheses following the words quoted.
2. Campbell, pp. 245-6.
3. Berlin, 1953, pp. 271-2.
4. Jung defines the regulatory motion of the libido in terms of *progression*, the forward swing which tends to unite the psyche with conscious demands, and *regression*, the backward swing toward unconscious needs. This movement may be seen as one aspect of Murphy's microcosmic quest.
5. In his essay on Beckett's style, *Die Unzulänglichkeit der Sprache* (Zürich, 1957), Niklaus Gessner points out the effect of such techniques: "Zuerst wird die eben beschriebene Handlung dadurch entwertet, dass sie ausdrücklich als Szene benannt wird und dann folgt noch eine Abschwächung . . . (p. 85).
6. See *L' Alittérature contemporaine* (Paris, 1958).
7. W. W. R. Ball, *Mathematical Recreations and Essays* (New York, 1939), quoted by George Gamov in *One Two Three . . . Infinity* (New York, 1947), p. 21. Lest this news should start a run on the market, it might be added that even if the priests move a disc every

97

second and work a 168-hour week, this cosmic permutation will require slightly more than 58,000,000,000,000 years to be completed.

II. Character

1. *Purgatorio*, IV, 110-111. For earlier appearances of this character in Beckett's work, see John Fletcher, *The Novels of Samuel Beckett* (London, 1964), pp. 13-37.
2. See Samuel I. Mintz, "Beckett's *Murphy*: A 'Cartesian' Novel," *Perspective*, XI, 3, pp. 156-165.
3. *Op. cit.*, *p. 54*.
4. See for example Ronald Gray, "*Waiting for Godot*: A Christian Interpretation," *Listener*, January 24, 1957, pp. 160-161, and Eric Bentley, "The Talent of Samuel Beckett," *New Republic*, May 14, 1956, pp. 20-21.
5. Warren Lee, "The Bitter Pill of Samuel Beckett," *Chicago Review*, X, 4, pp. 77-87.
6. The triangular dekad represented as ·∴∴· by which the Pythagoreans used to swear.
7. Cf. Proverbs, XXX, 15.
8. Cf. *Molloy* (New York, 1955), p. 75ff.

III. Symbol and Motif

1. *Op. cit.*
2. Letters to Beeckman of 26 March and 6 May 1618. Cf. Georges Poulet, *Etudes sur le temps humain* (Paris, 1949), p. 16.
3. Poulet, p. 26.
4. Poulet, p. 35.
5. Cf. Campbell, pp. 217-228.
6. On 7 October 1935 local apparent noon caught up with and passed zone time.
7. Vivian Robson, *A Beginner's Guide to Practical Astrology* (London, 1934), p. 13.
8. Myra Kingsley, *Outrageous Fortune* (New York, 1951), pp. 231-232.
9. A more limited and conventional use of the color may be observed in the early Beckett hero, Belacqua Shuah. In "Yellow" (*New World Writing*, New York, 1956, pp. 111-119) it is employed as a rather straightforward denotation for cowardice. Belacqua is hospitalized and fearfully awaiting surgery on his neck and toe; as he finally climbs onto the operating table, "his heart was running away, terrible yellow yerks in his skull."
10. For the Cartesian significance of heat in Murphy's garret, cf. Mintz, p. 161.

IV. Style

1. See the ten short stories published under the title of *More Pricks than Kicks* (London, 1934) and the collected poems, *Echo's Bones and Other Precipitates* (Paris, 1935).
2. Of this passage Gessner remarks "hin und wieder kann . . . eine der Gestalten Becketts in eine Lage geraten, wo er mit den festen Rede-

wendungen nicht mehr auskommt, und sich genötigt sieht, für einen Gedanken selber einen adäquaten Ausdruck zu suchen." *Op. cit.,* p. 55. [Now and then one of Beckett's characters can get caught in a spot where conventional patterns of discourse do not suffice, and find himself obliged to seek an adequate expression for a thought.]
3. Cf. Gessner, p. 107.
4. P. 49 [In the early work, *Murphy,* formulaic expressions are given directly to the speaking characters. The narrating subject does not yet use them himself.]
5. Gessner, p. 51.
6. P. 55. [the right word, which would become in the reader's mind a perception of the woman to be described, remains undiscoverable, and description can only be achieved with the aid of abstract numbers, through which it is once more illustrated that even in this area of expression; that is, in the area of description and representation, language is an inadequate medium.]
7. P. 60. [With Rabelais they were word explosions; it was uninhibited joy in the rediscovered uses and possibilities of language. With Beckett it has to do with making the useless word absurd. It is—as Beckett himself once said—the comic disparagement of the word.]
8. As Gessner points out, "diese Stellen sind dazu geeignet, den Glauben an die Sprache als selbstverständlichen Ausdruck zu erschüttern. Ebenso wie man die Illusion des Theaters zerstört, wenn man die Kulissen von hinten anschaut, ebenso will Beckett das Irreale und Fiktive der Sprache aufdecken, indem er in exhibitionistischer Manier zeigt—oder zu zeigen vergibt—"wie's gemacht wird." p. 66 [These places are designed to shake one's faith in language as unquestionable expression. Just as one destroys the illusion of the theatre when he looks from behind the curtains, so Beckett wishes to expose the unreal and fictive elements of language by revealing in an exhibitionistic manner—or pretending to reveal—"how it's done."]
9. Here Beckett's indebtedness to Joyce is apparent: "Richie, admiring, descanted on that man's glorious voice. He remembered one night long ago. Never forget that night. Si sang *'Twas rank and fame:* in Ned Lambert's 'twas. Good God he never heard in all his life a note like that he never did *then false one we had better part* so clear so God he never heard *since love lives not* a clinking voice ask Lambert he can tell you too.
"Goulding, a flush struggling in his pale, told Mr. Bloom, face of the night, Si in Ned Lambert's, Dedalus' house, sang *'Twas rank and fame.*
"He, Mr. Bloom, listened while he, Richie Goulding, told him, Mr. Bloom of the night he, Richie, heard him, Si Dedalus, sing *'Twas rank and fame* in his, Ned Lambert's house." (*Ulysses,* New York: 1961, pp. 276-277.)